Praise for _Exceptional M_
across the Autism Specti

"A dedicated teacher looks back on a long career working with students with autism. She presents a positive history of educators and leaders who improved our understanding of autism. There is also a great emphasis on developing a child's strengths and not becoming locked into labels."

TEMPLE GRANDIN author of _The Autistic Brain_ and _Thinking in Pictures_

"This is an exceptional book about exceptional minds by an exceptional teacher. It insightfully shares 40 years of practical day-to-day experience working in the trenches of the classroom, not the ivory tower. Those classrooms have been elementary and secondary, special education and regular with all ages and disabilities. The book properly promotes strength-based education, which focuses on needs, not labels. It advises how to "teach to the talent" and how to use handicaps or deficits as teaching opportunities. As a side benefit, it provides the history and evolution of autism spectrum disorder in as succinct a manner as any I have ever seen.

If I were to recommend one book on strength-based education to an established or beginning teacher in any public or private elementary or secondary classroom with special needs children with a variety of learning or other disabilities, this would be the book."

DAROLD A. TREFFERT, M.D. The Treffert Center for Exceptional Minds

Exceptional Minds across the Autism Spectrum

Exceptional Minds across the Autism Spectrum

Pathways to success in school and beyond

Corinne Levitt

GOLDENE KINDER PRESS

Cataloguing in publication information is available from Library and Archives Canada.
ISBN 978-1-7770589-0-6 (paperback)
ISBN 978-1-7770589-1-3 (ebook)

Some names and identifying details have been changed to protect the privacy of individuals.

Goldene Kinder Press

Produced by Page Two
www.pagetwo.com

Edited by Merrie-Ellen Wilcox
Copy edited by Melissa Edwards
Cover and interior design by Setareh Ashrafologhalai
Front cover painting by Eric Lewin
Back cover painting by David Lewin

20 21 22 23 24   5 4 3 2 1

It is with gratitude and admiration that I dedicate this book to Janis Rotman in recognition of her ongoing commitment to enriching the lives of countless children who are in need of our caring support and understanding. Many of her philanthropic projects at Holland Bloorview Kids Rehabilitation Hospital in Toronto, Canada, continue to provide families with the opportunity for their children to discover new interests and unrealized talents. Projects like the Spiral Garden, the drum circle, music therapy, or help from the Family Support Fund offer families reassurance and encouragement while facing challenging circumstances.

I am also grateful for Janis's generous sponsorship of this book. A fund has been established through the Jewish Community Foundation of Montreal, and all net proceeds from this book will be directed toward various autism programs and initiatives. I wish to thank Robert Kleinman and his team at the JCFM for their role in establishing this fund.

And to all the families, friends, teachers, and students who have helped make a difference . . . I will always be grateful.

When a trout rising to a fly gets hooked on a line and finds himself unable to swim about freely, he begins with a fight which results in struggles and splashes and sometimes an escape. Often, of course, the situation is too tough for him.

In the same way the human being struggles with his environment and with the hooks that catch him. Sometimes he masters his difficulties; sometimes they are too much for him. His struggles are all that the world sees and it naturally misunderstands them.

It is hard for a free fish to understand what is happening to a hooked one.

KARL A. MENNINGER

Contents

A Note on Terminology

Throughout this book, I use the labels that were in use at the time I'm describing to reflect the evolving nature of the terms and concepts. But in keeping with the current view of autism as part of a broad and multidimensional spectrum of traits, generally I use the term *autism spectrum disorder* (ASD), a concept first introduced in 1979 by British psychiatrist Lorna Wing and psychologist Judith Gould. Wing was always cautious about diagnostic labels, seeing them as useful only for getting people the services they needed. One of her favourite sayings, which she often repeated, captured this view: "Nature never draws a line without smudging it. You cannot separate into those 'with' and 'without' traits as they are so scattered... We need to see each child as an individual" (Rhodes 2011; *Telegraph* 2014). The inclusion of the term *spectrum* in the most recent edition of the *Diagnostic and Statistical Manual of Mental Disorders* (DSM-5, released in 2013) is a tribute to her foresight and wisdom as we continue to move a little closer to appreciating the complexities of the human mind and brain.

I will also use the term *neurotypical*, a label often used to describe individuals who are not on the spectrum. It is a term commonly used by people in the autism community to distinguish those who are not on the spectrum from themselves. *Neurotypical* and *typical* will be used interchangeably throughout the book.

A Note on Student Profiles

Names and identifying details of my students and their families have been changed to maintain confidentiality. Instead, I present composite student profiles based on experiences with students in various school settings. These profiles maintain similar learning styles while respecting the integrity of individual experiences. These profiles may remind you of individuals you know, or may prepare you for those you have yet to meet. In the case of students whose identity and work have been published, their names are included.

Introduction

OVER THE COURSE of nearly forty years of teaching in and around Toronto, Ontario, I have witnessed an interesting evolution in our attitudes toward "exceptional" students and how these attitudes affect our ability to help them reach their potential. More than money, resources, or teaching methods, it is largely our attitude toward those who may learn differently that determines their future opportunities; it is our attitude that shapes our vision.

Sometimes our attitude, despite our best intentions, falls short, and as a result our students do not receive the education they so justly deserve. But attitudes can change, and when that happens, we can move closer to understanding the struggles and challenges of individuals with exceptionalities.

My teaching experience has been wide and varied, for I believed that pursuing different teaching opportunities would broaden my understanding and help me become a more effective teacher. I started teaching in the mid-1970s and have since taught students of all ages and abilities. My background is in child development, adult education, linguistics, mental health, learning disabilities, strength-based teaching methods, and autism spectrum disorder. I have worked in both regular and special education settings at both the elementary and secondary levels, and have taught high school English to students at the academic level as well as at the basic level for those in need of more support. I've also taught special education qualifying courses for teachers at a faculty of education in Ontario, providing training in informal assessment along with techniques for developing meaningful education plans and approaches matched to student learning styles. These diverse and varied teaching experiences have allowed me to keep pace with the important educational changes that have taken place since the mid-1960s. I first realized the impact of these changes when I started teaching. Attitudes toward "exceptional" children were just beginning to change, as school boards would soon be legislated to accept *all* students with special needs in their schools (Bennett, Dworet, and Weber 2013).

The civil rights movement had encouraged parents of children with disabilities to advocate for their children's educational rights, and to educate the public about the benefits that can be realized when children are included as vital members of the community. Up until this time, children with exceptionalities had only discretionary access to public schools, and many were institutionalized, remained at home, or attended private programs. These parents played an important role in pushing open classroom doors for children previously excluded. The times, they were "a-changin'," and new legislation giving special needs children universal access to public education was on the horizon. (Legislation was first introduced in 1971 in England and Wales, and then in 1975 in the United States. Ontario, where I live, followed in 1980, after the other provinces.[1]) As a result of this new understanding and a recognition of the growing need to integrate children with handicaps as vital members of society, institutions that had isolated these children were starting to close.

Special education was still in its infancy when I began teaching, and autism was still a relatively rare and unfamiliar condition; it wasn't until 1980 that the term *autism* was included in the *Diagnostic and Statistical Manual* (DSM), and the number of children being identified with the disorder was still quite small. According to Bennett, Dworet, and Weber (2013, 180), "in the 1980s, prevalence rates for autism were held to be 4 in every 10,000. And for the most part, few people had any awareness, much less understanding, of the exceptionality, for many identified cases were institutionalized, often for life. By the end of the twentieth century, prevalence rates were being revised sharply upward to ranges of around 1 in every 1,000 births." Today the Centers for Disease Control and Prevention in the US sets the rate at 1 in 59.

Furthermore, at that time few educators were even aware of a recently identified neurological disorder called a "learning disability."[2] At first, this mysterious and invisible disorder seemed to affect a relatively small percentage of students, so it received little attention. But as awareness of this "new" condition continued to grow, the number of students being identified also began to increase. Parents played an important role in advocating for appropriate educational supports and inclusive placements in regular schools—not only at the elementary level but also, eventually, in high school and, later still, university. It was a revolutionary idea at the time, yet today we don't give it a second thought.

High school teachers like me were soon being hired to address this new educational challenge. In 1977, the largest school board in Canada asked me to help establish one of the first special education resource programs to be offered at the high school level. This was a big step forward, since many teachers still believed special education to be the sole responsibility of elementary schools; if the students hadn't been "cured" or "fixed" by adolescence, then they did not belong in a regular high school program. Yet by the time they reached high school age, many of these students were still struggling with the three Rs (Reading, wRiting and aRithmetic), along with the social and behavioural challenges, including run-ins with the law, that often accompany such difficulties. High school teachers and administrators were told that students with this invisible handicap were actually quite bright and simply learned differently, and that teaching methods would have to be adapted to accommodate their different styles of learning.

At first, high school teachers were skeptical of this new "hand-holding" approach to teaching, and worried that academic standards would be compromised by students who struggled with the basics, were socially awkward, and didn't seem to fit in. They believed classrooms would be disrupted and that "good" students would suffer. Some thought it was just another fad that would run its course: "Learning disabilities... What next?" was often heard in staff rooms as teachers resisted this challenge to the status quo.[3]

It was my job to support the students and their learning needs while trying to convince teachers to change their approaches and support this new direction in education. It was a good thing I was young and optimistic, for I was in for a bumpy ride. In fact, it would take almost fifteen years for teachers across North America and abroad to embrace this new understanding of learning. But gradually teachers and their students began to discover the hidden potential buried within this invisible handicap, and developed a deeper appreciation for different styles of learning.

The learning disabilities model of teaching recognizes that "the fundamental basis for all learning and for the potential for mislearning is neurological"[4] (Cruikshank 1980, 111). It also identifies strengths and interests, and develops individualized programs to help students reach their potential. Weaker skills are addressed by using students' strengths and personal learning styles; by identifying visual, auditory, or hands-on/sensory learning preferences, a more integrated and dynamic learning experience can be realized.

As an appreciation for different styles of learning began to develop, important educational changes soon followed, revolutionizing the well-established teaching methods of the time. The one-size-fits-all approach would eventually become a thing of the past. And as this new mindset continued to evolve, we witnessed the dramatic impact this changed view had on student success; where previously the system came close to giving up on "weak" students, now educators were taking notice as these students began to achieve and flourish. Students, of course, would play an important role in the slow and difficult process of allaying educators' fears and misconceptions about learning disabilities—once they were finally given a chance to display their strengths, no longer invisible or hidden from view.

Looking back, I realize that many of my high school students with learning disabilities also presented with various autistic traits. But we had little awareness of autism spectrum disorders in those years; we would not even become aware of Hans Asperger's work until 1981, when Lorna Wing published her paper, "Asperger's Syndrome: A Clinical Account." The first official English translation of Asperger's work, by

Uta Frith, became available only ten years later. And it wasn't until 1994 that the term *Asperger's syndrome* was included in the DSM, with the publication of the DSM-IV. (The term was folded into the autism spectrum in the DSM-5, published in 2013.)

But regardless of the labels, it was the *neurological understanding* of learning that enabled the success of many of my students over the course of my teaching career.

Anthony: A Student Teaches Us a Valuable Lesson

Anthony was a fourteen-year-old Grade 9 student who would soon help his high school teachers re-examine their preconceived ideas about hidden abilities and educational "standards."

When Anthony first arrived at his new school, in the late 1970s, his teachers saw a student who was struggling with his courses, failing history and English, and receiving special education resource room support for a few hours each week. They noticed he rarely made eye contact, was physically and socially awkward, had sensory issues with respect to noise, was reluctant to speak in class, and had difficulty writing things down and staying on task, with a tendency toward hyperactivity. His teachers questioned whether he was ready for high school and wondered if he should have been held back in Grade 8 for another year, for it was believed that an academic high school was not the appropriate place to learn the basics or receive remedial support.

Anthony's parents reported that he seemed more comfortable in the company of adults than with his own peers, and as a child had spoken late and was physically awkward. But they noticed that, around the age of four, he suddenly made up for his language delay and showed remarkable strength in the areas of reading and verbal expression, despite his ongoing difficulty demonstrating these abilities in writing. As well, Anthony had many hobbies, including assembling stereo equipment from commercial kits, and a love of music.

It wasn't until adolescence, at the insistence of his parents, that Anthony received his first formal psychoeducational assessment from the school board, in order to determine which high school program would best meet his needs. The report indicated that Anthony had a previously unidentified learning disability and above-average intelligence, even though he had experienced much failure throughout elementary and middle school and barely passed Grade 8. In spite of this new information and the diagnosis identifying Anthony's high level of intelligence, his parents still wondered if an academic high school was appropriate, as his uneven learning profile presented something of a paradox. (Looking back, I recognize that Anthony had that "little professor" air about him, a term Asperger had used in his seminal paper on the syndrome later named after him. But of course, we didn't yet know about Asperger's work.)

Nevertheless, the term *learning disability* would serve Anthony's needs quite well. Anthony was given access to the special education resource room, where we could address his learning needs in conjunction with his courses of study. During our sessions there, I encouraged Anthony to focus on his verbal strengths, to dictate his answers into a tape recorder in a quiet and private setting where he could relax and also transcribe his thoughts and ideas into written form, thereby demonstrating his true abilities to his teachers. (Anthony's writing was almost illegible, so he typed his work whenever possible. Those were the days of typewriters and Wite-Out; today, computer programs like Dragon Dictate work quite well in this regard.)

One day, Anthony's history teacher came to see me, showing me his latest assignment. Rather than being pleased with his progress, she appeared quite upset; she believed Anthony had cheated in light of the poor quality of his previous handwritten assignments and his reticence to speak in class. She couldn't understand how he could possibly be capable of producing this high-calibre work, given his difficulty with basic skills. I played Anthony's tape for her and she was impressed by what she heard. Could this be the same student? What magic had I performed? But there was no magic—I had just given Anthony the opportunity to demonstrate his abilities and let his strengths shine through.

A two-dollar cassette tape, an old typewriter, and a change in mindset helped redirect Anthony's educational path toward university and success. His teacher's new ability to see his strengths instead of his deficits helped her understand him and his previously hidden abilities. The experience also helped her question her preconceived views about learning disabilities, learning styles, and intelligence.

Anthony's teacher became a strong ally and suggested that I speak at the next staff meeting to help other teachers understand more about different styles of learning and the implications for teaching. From that day forward, Anthony was able to further not only his own education but the education of his teachers as well.

A Shift in Mindset

An amazing educational transformation began to take place in our schools, beyond what we could possibly have imagined at the time. And it was all because our students with learning disabilities responded so well to this new, neurologically informed approach to teaching and learning. Our students' progress exceeded our expectations and taught us an important lesson about the value to be found in different ways of thinking and experiencing the world. Educators and researchers took notice and began to move away from the limited view of simply addressing deficits, taking a deeper look into the thinking patterns and perceptual abilities of these interesting and capable students. They wondered if their success might have important implications with respect to current teaching approaches for *all* students.

The experience taught us that understanding neurological challenges serves to broaden our teaching abilities—and our ability to enhance the learning potential of everyone—as we continue in our efforts to explore and learn more about the inner workings of the human brain. And I believe that this understanding, and the neurologically informed approach to teaching, opens up even more possibilities for students on the spectrum.

As I continued working as a high school special education resource teacher throughout the 1980s, the demand for effective teaching approaches and better teacher training continued to transform our understanding of the word *exceptional*: exceptional was no longer the exception, but instead the rule for best practices in teaching for all students. I continued to broaden my experience and understanding by taking advantage of new teaching opportunities that were now being offered in a variety of settings. I worked with mental health professionals in a facility-based classroom for adolescents diagnosed with schizophrenia, helping students earn their English high school credits as they prepared to return to their regular schools. Later, from 1991 to 1998, I headed a special education program at a high school for adults, providing support for students with a variety of challenges, including brain injuries, mental health concerns, physical disabilities, visual or hearing impairments, and learning disabilities. Many of these students had either missed out on receiving special education support when they were younger, or had suffered an injury and needed upgraded skills to help them adapt and find suitable employment. Little was known about autism in the adult population at that time, but I now realize that many of the students we worked with were on the spectrum. Nevertheless, a strength-based approach to addressing our students' needs ensured that everyone received the appropriate help. Although very successful, the program was cancelled in the late 1990s because of a lack of funding—and the view that education for adults with special needs was no longer a priority. And we had come so far…

Toward the end of the 1990s, I returned to teaching adolescents at a regular high school, as head of the special education department. After almost a decade of working with adults, I saw that a significant change had taken place, as a greater number of students being identified with ASD were now attending secondary school. And as the number of students with ASD was steadily increasing, so were the challenges facing well-meaning educators, challenges not unlike what we experienced when students with learning disabilities first made us question many of our preconceived ideas about deficits, abilities, intelligence, and different kinds of minds.

As I began working with my students on the spectrum, I recognized a growing need to improve educational opportunities for students who learned differently but were often still misunderstood. And I began to realize how helpful my background in learning disabilities would be as I embraced this new and important educational opportunity. Meanwhile, encouraged by lobbying efforts in the United States, and the passage there in 1990 of the Individuals with Disabilities Education Act (where, for the first time, autism was "classified as a disability for purposes of entitlements"), parents continued to advocate on behalf of their children.[5]

At the same time, though, many vocational programs were starting to close. This was most unfortunate, as such programs would have provided another option for students on the spectrum who displayed talents and abilities in the trades and enjoyed hands-on learning, while also giving them a chance to find meaningful employment. (Today we are facing a shortage of skilled labour—a terrible loss for individuals, our community, and the economy. Another lost opportunity.)

Traditional high schools would now have to play catch-up as they tried to meet the needs of this new and still unfamiliar group of students. Small segregated (now referred to as "congregated") high schools for students with developmental challenges and/or autism spectrum disorder were being established, and a few years later I accepted a job at one of these schools to familiarize myself with the different educational options available to students with ASD. I wanted to learn more about best practices and outcomes in order to better prepare my students for the future.

As I continued to observe various programs and approaches for students on the spectrum, regardless of the setting or school level, I was surprised to discover that a greater emphasis was often being placed on students' deficits and what they couldn't do, rather than on their strengths. This ran contrary to what the previous few decades had taught us about the neurological nature of different styles of learning; somehow, this understanding did not seem to include students on the spectrum. How easily we forget the lessons from the past when facing yet another new and unfamiliar challenge in education! But I held fast to what I knew to be true, knowing that my background in learning disabilities and strength-based teaching was exactly what my students needed.

During the last few decades, we public school educators have witnessed a sea change in our understanding of the learning process, and have come to realize that a neurologically based view of different thinking patterns and learning styles is so effective that it should no longer be limited to students with learning disabilities—now, it is considered to be the gold standard of instruction for *all* students. "Differentiated instruction," also known as "universal design," [6] based on an appreciation of varied and diverse patterns of thinking, has now replaced the one-size-fits-all teaching methods of the past.

So why hasn't this understanding been extended to students on the spectrum, who also learn differently? Like learning disabilities, ASD is recognized as a neurological condition, so why is the neurologically informed approach not being used with students who stand to benefit the most from these techniques and practices? As I continued to teach my students with ASD, it seemed that educators had lost confidence in their ability to meet the needs of students they wanted to help but still did not understand.

The Students Were Ready for School, but Were the Schools Ready for the Students?[7]

To address the growing number of students with ASD in high schools, public educators turned to health-care agencies (and the medical model) for advice and direction, just as the elementary schools had done years earlier. Teachers would now be expected to rely on expertise from outside their classrooms, and from professionals with no background or experience in teaching or pedagogy. The medical model focuses on "treating" deficits and behaviours, and on what the child can't do rather than on what the child can do. Learning needs are put on hold until the "behaviour" is under control; a greater focus on *treating* "what's wrong" rather than on *teaching* "what could be better" (Grandin and Panek 2013, 180-81) overshadows the educational expectations teachers would otherwise have for their students.

Ontario's special education handbook for teachers raises this ongoing concern, not only describing what is experienced by many Ontario public school teachers, but also reflecting what is taking place in many public schools across North America and beyond:

> Very often a student identified with an ASD comes to the classroom with a treatment program already in place. The teacher—and the EA if the classroom is fortunate enough to have one—is then expected to adhere to the tenets of that program and sometimes even be in charge of implementing it whether or not the teacher or EA agree with its principles or have received training in it … As well, especially in inclusive classrooms, a method with laid on requirements has the potential of denying the purpose of inclusion by isolating the student, however unintentionally. On the other hand, teachers can be just as confused and challenged by a student with ASD as anyone else, and the clear plan of response typically outlined in a treatment program may well be a relief. (Bennett et al. 2019, 210)

Unfortunately, the role and expertise of the teacher in all of these scenarios has been compromised and diminished, along with the benefits to be had from a meaningful educational experience.

The reliance on outside professionals for advice and direction—the medical model—has further limited the need for public educators to explore meaningful and effective educational approaches for students on the spectrum. I realized I needed to learn more and went searching for resources, and I soon discovered a treasure-trove of material by leading educators and researchers in the field of autism. Their work confirmed that I was on the right path. Moreover, I was surprised to find that several of these excellent teaching models had been available since the 1960s, yet teachers like me, with a solid background in special education, knew little about them. Throughout this book, I will highlight these contributions, made by the pioneers in the field of autism who have inspired me and who have offered the educational insights I was seeking; they are the true champions, advocating for the valuable and transformative role education can have in the lives of individuals with ASD. Their methods are practical and inexpensive, and can easily be adapted to any teaching situation. Their work has informed my own teaching methods with promising results.

Many professionals still believe the early years offer the only opportunity for intervention to bring about meaningful change for children on the spectrum. However, research and best practices demonstrate that adolescence offers yet another important and critical stage in brain development for learning and developing new skills and talents, less rigid compensatory behaviours, and improved social development and workplace skills. This important window of opportunity offers a second chance at harnessing emerging abilities and unrealized talents and interests through appropriate educational interventions and job-related experiences (e.g., co-op education). In addition, adolescents are more motivated when offered the chance to pursue and develop their particular areas of interest as part of an appropriate learning or work experience.

My work with adolescents not only focused my attention on developing their full potential, but also offered the chance to look back at their early years, providing me with a more complete understanding of their learning experiences. While this vantage offers insights for students of all ages and levels of ability, it also provides an opportunity to review past and current practices as we prepare for better outcomes. It is important to remember that special education methods and approaches developed for "exceptional" students in the past can be viewed as the midwife for the "differentiated" strength-based learning model now being promoted throughout North America and around the world for *all* students. But the most important lessons to be learned are from the students themselves. From the very beginning, my students taught me that a strength-based approach can reveal abilities and talents previously hidden or misunderstood, and that, as strengths and interests develop, challenging behaviours begin to recede.

Throughout the pages of this book, you will meet students like Ellen, who stopped having meltdowns when things didn't go according to plan and instead learned how to handle changes and disruptions. Ellen loved lists and schedules, and applied those skills to following recipes and her passion for baking. She eventually found employment at a co-operative catering business for special needs adults. And Lauren, who once had difficulty interacting with other students and kept to herself until she was taught how to read as an adolescent. Everything changed when she discovered the world of Harry Potter. After starting a fan club at school, she made many new friends who also shared her passion. There's Larry, who was about to be suspended from school but whose behaviour improved once he was enrolled in a more challenging credit program, in line with his level of ability and interest in computers. He eventually found employment working as an assistant computer programmer in a photography lab. And

Hakim, who hardly spoke but, with support, found employment at Tim Hortons. Tally turned an obsession with pulling at threads into a talent for knitting, eventually selling her work. Fred, who was passionate about the subway transit system, found work as a courier for a company dedicated to helping adults with special needs. There's Kenny, who discovered his voice after joining the community choir. And Ravi, who wrote in his student newspaper, "We are capable of more than we are credited with and if you take a moment to notice, you will see us and all we can do."

You will also discover the heart of a poet in Eric, whose poem was published in a prestigious public library magazine. Eric is also a talented artist, and it is his colourful painting that is beautifully presented on the cover of this book—he was inspired by our school garden, and by one of his favourite artists, Claude Monet. Eric's younger brother, David, who was in a similar program at the same school, is also a talented artist. One of his drawings, "The Secret Garden," is on the back cover, and it invites you to follow the path of our school garden and explore its secrets and hidden treasures.

My interest in advancing the strengths of *exceptional* and *extraordinary* students has never wavered, and it fuels my desire to share what I've learned. The result is the book you now hold in your hands. It shows what lies at the heart of my teaching philosophy, so that others might benefit and enhance their own understanding and practices as we continue to learn from each other.

Different Kinds of Minds

Temple Grandin has had a huge influence on my development as a teacher, and her research and insights dovetail with my own philosophy of teaching. A distinguished professor of animal science at Colorado State University and one of the world's leading experts in the design of humane livestock handling facilities, she is also a well-known autism advocate and author of many landmark books describing her experiences living an accomplished and meaningful life with autism. She is a popular international speaker, advocating for a deeper understanding of ASD and different kinds of minds. Her life has been portrayed in the award-winning movie *Temple Grandin* (2010).

One of Grandin's recent books, *The Autistic Brain: Thinking across the Spectrum* (2013), presents fascinating scientific research that challenges teachers, parents, and health-care professionals to look past behaviours to gain a deeper understanding of ASD and different kinds of minds. The section on learning styles is extremely important for teachers and reinforces how well-suited my experience in learning disabilities was to meeting the needs of my students. But Grandin also recognizes the ongoing challenge facing educators today. Even when we think we are focusing on strengths, and even with the best of intentions, we unwittingly slip back to focusing on behaviours and weaknesses:

> I'm certainly not saying we should lose sight of the need to work on deficits. But as we've seen, the focus on deficits is so intense and so automatic that people lose sight of the strengths. Just yesterday I spoke to the director of a school for autistic children and she mentioned that the school tries to match a student's strengths with internship or employment opportunities in the neighborhood. But when I asked how they identified the strengths, she immediately started talking about how they helped overcome social deficits. If even experts can't stop thinking about *what's wrong* instead of *what could be better*, how can anyone expect the families

who are dealing with autism on a daily basis to think any differently? (180-81)

My book is, in part, a response to the challenge that Grandin has set before us—to stop, reflect and re-examine what lies behind our own understanding of ASD and the way it impacts our expectations and how we truly see and relate to each other.

In 2010, Temple Grandin was recognized as one of *Time* magazine's 100 most influential people in the world. This book will try to honour that by demonstrating how her influence and expertise can be realized in every school, classroom, and community. After all, the classroom is where students spend most of their day and where meaningful growth and development can take place. Creating a culture of respect and dignity for students with special needs is fundamental for promoting social inclusion and supportive communities. Providing better training for teachers and educators along with developing a deeper understanding and sensitivity to the challenges of special needs students will go a long way toward fostering real change.

I often think of a particular image that Grandin describes in her book *Thinking in Pictures: My Life with Autism*, for it reminds me of my own students and their path toward success. She quotes from her personal diary and describes how she often relies on visualizing a door to help her transition to what lies ahead (2006, 18): "I am often asked what the single breakthrough was that enabled me to adapt to autism. There was no single breakthrough. It was a series of incremental improvements. My diary entries show very clearly that I was fully aware that when I mastered one door, it was only one step in a whole series."

I like to think of this book as the "door" to my classroom, which, once opened, will allow you to experience a new way of seeing things in "a series of incremental improvements." My book is your introduction to the experiences of many of the extraordinary students I've known throughout my years of teaching and will provide you with an opportunity to follow in their footsteps. Telling their stories and recounting their experiences is my way of thanking them for their trust, patience, and understanding as I muddled my way through the important lessons they taught me and which we can all value. I invite you to walk through my classroom door and follow us with open hearts and minds. Welcome!

Rethinking Education

Education Is Key

When I retired from teaching, I was working in a small special education public high school for students with developmental needs and autistic tendencies. Shortly before my last day of teaching, as I began packing my teaching materials into a couple of banker's boxes, I was approached by colleagues asking for any resources I might pass along to help them meet the needs of their students. I explained that the materials on their own would not prove very helpful, as it was the mindset and understanding that would achieve the best results. I emphasized how important it was to take time to listen to and observe what our students were trying to communicate, to discover their strengths, and to follow their lead.

In the following few chapters, I will outline the lessons I learned and the techniques I developed with my students as we navigated our way through the spectrum and beyond. I will also explain the learning theories behind my teaching methods, which are supported by important research in cognitive development, psycholinguistics, and neuroscience. My goal as a special education teacher has always been driven by a commitment to developing a meaningful and enriched learning experience for my students beyond just focusing on coping strategies and managing behaviours. More importantly, I see the high school years as another important opportunity to focus on developing students' strengths and interests in order to ensure that, upon graduation, they are able to find meaningful work or a program that will allow them to continue to develop their abilities and talents.

Student success often relies on the effective and nuanced implementation of teaching methods by educators who continue to challenge their students by asking, "What's next?" This recognizes the dynamic nature of lifelong learning. Our work is never done, for there is always a next step and new challenges to be met.

ASKING THE RIGHT QUESTIONS

- How do we identify and encourage strengths and "teach to the talent"?

- For what future outcomes are we preparing our students?

- How can we help and prepare students who are able to continue with post-secondary education?

- What other opportunities (jobs, co-op placements, apprenticeships, community programs, nonprofit start-up initiatives, etc.) are available if students can't continue with post-secondary education?

1

The Acting Self versus the Thinking Self

*If you want to know what the symptoms of autism mean,
you have to go beyond the behavior of the autistic person and
into his or her brain. But wait. Isn't the diagnosis of autism
based on behaviors? Isn't our whole approach to autism
a result of what the experience looks like from the outside
(the acting self) rather than what the experience feels like from
the inside (the thinking self)? Yes. Which is why I believe
the time has come to rethink the autistic brain.*

TEMPLE GRANDIN
The Autistic Brain: Thinking across the Spectrum

TEACHING APPROACHES and theories that focus primarily on student deficits and behaviours—the "acting self"—rather than on a true understanding of the "thinking self" tend to prevent us from looking beyond behaviours and into the hearts and minds of students with autism spectrum disorder. Neurological challenges and consequential behaviours are dynamic and pervasive in nature yet respond beautifully when an appreciation for the individual and diverse patterns of thinking and perceiving are understood and addressed as an important and integral part of an effective and dynamic educational program. We now understand the neurological nature of autism, but still tend to focus on students' behaviours and deficits before considering learning needs. During the various stages of child development, it is important to see all the moving parts of our dynamic nature as interconnected aspects of what makes us tick; developmental challenges or "detours" can then be understood as interconnected and complex aspects of cognitive, sensory, and social experiences and their impact on development.

Often, without thinking, we tend to start with what we can observe. But as Temple Grandin has wisely pointed out, we should not allow ourselves to be sidelined by behaviours and to forget the "thinking self." Being socially withdrawn or hampered by communication difficulties is where people with ASD end up, not where they begin. Lorna Wing (1979, 11) emphasized that these challenges should be considered more "a consequence of a defect in the cognitive skills underlying the development of social communication, symbolic language and complex verbal reasoning." It is not "what comes first, the chicken or the egg?"—*it is both*. Think of it as a more integrated approach, rather than one that simply addresses discrete symptoms on a checklist.

Looking at behaviours in isolation, without an appreciation for learning strengths, perceptual styles of processing information, and sensory challenges, can only result in a very simplistic and limited understanding of different minds and their complexities. By "thinking across the spectrum," Grandin invites us to take a closer look and offers a much-needed lesson in developing our own understanding as we continue to act in the best interests of our students.

Once behaviours are viewed as windows through which we can observe patterns of thinking, and are understood as responses to sensory or perceptual experiences, much can be learned. Suddenly a "behaviour" can be worked with, and can even be developed into a strength, rather than be extinguished. Once we begin to see things differently, from the inside out, rather than just from the outside in, and as we begin to understand the perspective of the "thinking self," everything changes—mindset, misconceptions, and what is now possible.

TEMPLE GRANDIN

TEMPLE GRANDIN has led an *extra-ordinary* life, for she is an *extra-ordinary* individual. Now in her seventies, she continues to realize her dreams as she juggles three demanding careers, all an expression of her commitment to improving the lives of animals and of people with autism spectrum disorder. A well-respected professor of animal science at Colorado State University, Grandin specializes in animal behaviour, a discipline she helped establish as a result of her early research and her interest in the behavioural effects of cattle chutes on animals. (Cattle chutes are used to secure the animals during inoculation, branding, or castration; the gentle pressure applied from panels exerts a calming effect to help the animals relax.) Extending her expertise in this new field of research, Grandin developed a very successful second career designing humane livestock-handling facilities around the world for companies including McDonald's, Burger King, Wendy's, and KFC.

Grandin's fascination with cattle chutes and their impact on animal behaviour stemmed from a discovery she made about herself and her own challenges with autism during a high school summer vacation spent at her aunt Ann's farm in Arizona. At first, Grandin had resisted her mother's wish for her to spend the summer away, preferring to stay close to home and continue following the familiar routine of her special boarding school. Grandin had difficulty adjusting to new environments and people, but with the support and encouragement of her mother and aunt she reluctantly agreed to go. It was not an easy adjustment, but Grandin grew to love life on the ranch, helping out with chores, discovering new routines, and demonstrating a real talent for creating innovative ranch projects. Her designs were both artistic and creative, from silver-mounted bridles to a full-sized gate with weights and pulleys that could be opened from the car by simply pulling a rope.

During this enriching summer experience, Grandin also began to develop a keen interest in animals and became curious about their behaviour and inner lives. Her aunt encouraged these interests as she came to appreciate her niece's unconventional way of experiencing the world. Grandin enjoyed spending time with the animals, often preferring their company to people's. She became fascinated by the squeeze chutes and their calming effect on cattle, wondering if such gentle pressure might help with her own challenges with fear and anxiety. One memorable day, with the help of her hesitant but understanding aunt, Grandin decided to climb into the cattle chute and found the answer she was looking for: "The squeeze chute provided relief from my nerve attacks. True to form, I became fixated on it" (Grandin and Scariano 2005, 95).

This experience was a key that helped unlock Grandin's understanding of herself and subsequently changed the direction of her life. Her true talents were unleashed that summer. And there was no holding her back—she hit her stride and has never stopped.

Today, Temple Grandin is regarded as one of the world's leading experts in the field of autism spectrum disorder. The passion she brings to her third career—or calling—demonstrates an unwavering need to improve the quality of life for individuals on the autism spectrum as well as for their families. Grandin's important work as an autism advocate began in 1986, with the publication of her autobiography, *Emergence: Labeled Autistic*, which offered the world one of the first personal accounts of living with autism. (At the time, Grandin was completing her doctorate and working as one of the first successful livestock handling equipment designers in the world.) This was groundbreaking! Her insights provided a different understanding of autism, a condition still shrouded in mystery, misunderstanding, and heartbreak. Most importantly, she offered new hope and a chance to imagine a way to achieve a meaningful life with autism. In her story (Grandin and Scariano 2005, 9), she challenged us to broaden our understanding, asking, "How is it possible that a young child whose parents were told she might have to live her life in an institution can confound the 'experts'? How does a child, labeled autistic, emerge into the real world?"

During Grandin's early years, her mother, Eustacia Cutler, recognized that something was not quite right; her daughter was not like other children her age. Even as a six-month-old baby, she had begun to resist being held in her mother's arms. Then she began to display many of the classic symptoms of autism: Grandin (1986, 24) tells us she developed "a fixation on spinning objects, a preference to be alone, destructive behavior, temper tantrums, inability to speak, sensitivity to sudden noises, appearance of deafness, and my intense interest in odors."

But Grandin's mother held firm in her belief that her daughter could learn, thrive, and overcome many of her challenges. Dr. Bronson Caruthers, a neurologist who understood the neurological nature of autism, in contrast to the prevalent but misguided view of the time, which blamed the mother, offered Cutler the support she was seeking. By the of age two, Grandin was still not speaking, and Caruthers recommended speech lessons. Following his advice, Cutler found "Mrs. Reynolds's little school for children who . . . had trouble speaking (templegrandineustaciacutlerautism fund.com)." This experience not only helped Grandin learn to talk, but also encouraged all of the children at the school to be part of a group, learning to wait, listen, take turns, and play together. In such an enriched setting, words and language came to be shared and valued. By age five and a half, Grandin had found her voice. She was well on her way and would have much to tell us.

Early on, Cutler saw that a meaningful education could help her daughter develop her potential as an active member in family and community life. At home, she encouraged her daughter to actively participate, involving her in daily chores, routines, and, of course, fun and games, both inside and outside the home. Grandin joined neighbourhood children at play, at community events, and in programs and activities. There would be no sitting on the sidelines, watching life pass them by.

It was not an easy journey; there were many challenges along the way. But a child who had been "labelled autistic," who didn't learn to speak until the age of five and a half, eventually found her voice and her passion.

GRANDIN 1986 Grandin and Scariano 2005; Temple Grandin & Eustacia Cutler Autism Fund 2017; Cutler 2004

Ain't Misbehavin'

In the groundbreaking book *Animals Make Us Human: Creating the Best Life for Animals* (2010), Temple Grandin, along with co-author Catherine Johnson, offers helpful advice for pet owners, farmers, livestock handlers, and even zookeepers. Yet, as the title reflects, Grandin's insights have far-reaching implications for human behaviour as well. Her findings not only made me aware of the misperceptions and misunderstandings I had about our family cat, they also helped me realize and appreciate how much our environment impacts both animal and human behaviour, and how changes to that environment can elicit more positive outcomes for all of us.

"Slaughterhouses: A Jungle No More," published in the *Economist* in October 2015, describes how Temple Grandin's designs have reformed the meat industry.

economist.com/ node/21671150/print

It is Grandin's expertise in the study of animal behaviour and her unique and, yes, empathic understanding of how much the environment helps shape animal and human responses that has enriched our understanding of ASD at such a profound level. But now we must take that understanding to the classroom so that its influence can be realized each and every day in the lives of our students.

Grandin helped me develop a new understanding of behaviour, and I soon realized that I would need to look at behaviour, the environment, and teaching a little differently. I would need to figure out not just *what* was wrong but, more importantly, *why* it was wrong in order to design an effective and meaningful classroom *learning* environment for my students. Many of these changes are easy to implement and are based on common sense; the challenge, however, is getting professionals to think about the *why* together with the *what*.

As educators, we must now understand the importance of facilitating changes in a student's environment in order to address the causes of concerning behaviours. There is still a tendency to focus on changing the child rather than addressing the sensory and perceptual challenges that impact the child within their environment; we must keep reminding ourselves that the behaviours are more a consequence of the environment than simply a feature of ASD. The chicken-and-egg dynamic can sometimes cloud our ability to tease cause from effect, but Grandin's research demonstrates clearly where the true problems exist; we need to look at the outside world and its influence on the child's responses, with our focus resting not solely on the child but rather on the many influences that can shape responses and behaviours. When square pegs are able to fit nicely into round holes that have been broadened and modified, there is much less friction and far less wear and tear on the pegs.

Hakim: "Noises Off"

Temple Grandin (2010, 3) wrote, "My theory is that the environment animals live in should activate their positive emotions as much as possible, and not activate their negative emotions more than necessary. If we get the animal's emotions right, we will have fewer problem behaviors." This statement can apply equally to the classroom environment.

A normally calm and quiet student of mine, Hakim, became agitated when our classroom was disrupted by support staff who wanted to use the laundry facilities in a connected room. Not only did this intrusion interrupt our class, but we were also subjected to the unpredictable sound of the dryer's BUZZZZZZZ!!!!!! as it reached the end of the cycle. The jarring sound upset the entire class, but it created a particularly high level of anxiety and upset for Hakim. He loved music and had perfect pitch, and seemed especially sensitive to annoying sounds, such as chairs scraping across a tiled floor. We placed tennis balls on the legs of our chairs, which easily solved that problem. The dryer problem, on the other hand, presented more of a challenge.

I had tried to arrange for access to the laundry room to occur outside of class hours, but to no avail. My request was not taken seriously, as clean kitchen towels were needed for the school cafeteria. Hakim's problem was not considered to be that serious; his reaction was viewed as typical autistic behaviour. It was suggested that perhaps Hakim could simply wear headphones when the laundry facilities were in use. I explained that headphones weren't appropriate for this situation, as we were *all* bothered by the noise and disruption, but I was told that many Individual Education Plans recommend the use of headphones for students with sound sensitivities, and this situation was no different. Hakim was sixteen and had never used headphones before, and I worried that introducing headphones at this stage of his life might actually heighten his sensitivity and create more problems in the long run. He'd managed quite well until the dryer situation had presented itself. Hakim's response to the buzzer was actually quite understandable.

I too was annoyed by the dryer's jarring buzzer. It often frayed my nerves and disrupted my own train of thought. More importantly, it interfered with our learning, and with the positive classroom environment I worked hard to establish. Once that buzzer went off, our learning potential for the rest of the day was compromised.

When I was teaching Grade 12 English in a traditional high school, my class would *never* have been interrupted by support staff carrying out laundry duties. It is simply not done.

Was the teaching in my class with special needs students of any less value? Did people believe our job was more caretaking than helping students learn and find their place in society before they must leave, at the age of twenty-one? There was important learning taking place and much work to be done. The situation was unacceptable, as was the attitude that went with it. Too often, special education programs are reactive rather than proactive, with a tendency to respond to situations only when they become problematic. In the long run, this ends up creating more problems than it solves. We must take full advantage of the time our students spend in school to honour their right to an education. Parents fought long and hard to achieve universal access for students with disabilities, which means access to a proper education and not merely access to the building.

When the support staff arrived with their baskets of laundry, long before we even heard the sound of the dreaded buzzer, Hakim would begin to show signs of distress, immediately getting out of his chair and pacing back and forth at the back of the classroom. It was clear that he was no longer able to focus on his schoolwork, and this was unacceptable to me as his teacher.

Since I had rejected headphones as the solution to this problem, I realized I would have to find a creative solution on my own. So, with the help of another staff member and a handy Robertson screwdriver, the buzzer was silenced forever. Peace and quiet was finally restored to our classroom, and Hakim was able to continue with his schoolwork.

Unfortunately, I was less successful in preventing the disruptive interruptions from the support staff. Change doesn't always come as quickly as we would like. While I was able to find a partial solution by silencing the buzzer, I realized that we faced a far more serious problem with respect to heightening awareness about the sensory issues that can and do compromise the learning environment for students with ASD. And there is an even greater need to raise awareness about the value of education in the lives of our students. While headphones can be effective in certain situations, they should be used with care and common sense. When overused, they can further isolate students and limit opportunities for social interaction and meaningful communication, the very things we wish to encourage. Our goal should be to use such strategies less and less as we help our students adapt to their surroundings. But first we must recognize the cause of the problem and consider how much the environment impacts student learning. Misdirected solutions that focus solely on "behaviour" may work in the short term, but end up creating more problems, as well as limiting rather than enhancing learning potential. We all need to adapt if a change for the better is to be realized.

As Temple Grandin reminds us in her first book, *Emergence: Labeled Autistic* (2005, 146), "The principle is to work with the animal's behavior instead of against it. I think the same principle applies to autistic children—work with them instead of against them. Discover their hidden talents and develop them."

Hakim graduated a few years later and found a part-time job at Tim Hortons. With the help of a supportive and understanding employer, he is happy and successful. He loves listening to the music in the background and often sings along while he works.

Gordon and Linda: Theory of Heart

I must admit that the amount of attention Temple Grandin gave to the emotional life of animals in *Animals Make Us Human* surprised me. I hadn't expected this from a person with autism. My apologies. Over the years, we have been hearing about "theory of mind" and the difficulty people with autism have understanding the feelings and thoughts of others, and yet here was this incredible book describing the emotions behind the behaviour of animals. How was this possible?

My own "theory of mind" with respect to animals was weak and impaired until Grandin provided me with a completely different view of how animals experience their environment. In addition, Grandin's account of her own experiences with autism and sensory issues helped broaden and deepen my understanding of the importance of creating a positive learning environment for my students.

During my years of teaching, I never found my students to be lacking in empathy; they may have difficulty figuring out what is wrong, as we all do from time to time, but they certainly show concern and awareness when someone is upset. One day one of my students, Linda, who was usually quite happy, suddenly burst into tears. Gordon, a fifteen-year-old who kept to himself and rarely spoke, quickly ran over with a box of tissues and said, "It will be okay." He remained at Linda's side until she smiled and accepted the tissues. She thanked him and that seemed to do the trick. We never figured out why Linda was upset, but Gordon had things in hand and all was well once again.

Sometimes it's hard to figure out why people are upset, but if we know or at least try to make things a little better—well, that works for me.

By considering the emotion behind behaviour, we are better able to address real needs. As we begin to rethink our understanding of "behaviour," new opportunities emerge, which we otherwise might have missed.

DIG IT

I ALWAYS loved gerbils as a child; I watched them with fascination and marvelled at their industrious nature. Temple Grandin's account of gerbil behaviour in *Animals Make Us Human* gave me a much deeper appreciation for what drives animal behaviour and how this understanding can actually apply to all of us, and especially to people with ASD:

> A really good study on whether animals have purely behavioral needs was done with gerbils. Gerbils love to dig and tunnel, and a lot of them develop a corner-digging stereotypy when they're around thirty days old. A *stereotypy* is an abnormal repetitive behavior (ARB for short), such as a lion or tiger pacing back and forth in its cage for hours on end. Pets and farm animals can develop stereotypies, too. Stereotypies are defined as abnormal behaviors that are repetitive, invariant (lions always pace the same path in their cages), and seemingly pointless...
>
> [R]esearchers have hypothesized that the reason captive gerbils develop stereotypic digging is that they have a biological need to dig that they can't express inside a cage... [I]n nature gerbils don't dig just to be digging. Once they've hollowed out their underground home, they stop digging. Maybe what the gerbils need is the result of the digging, not the behavior itself... the motivation for a gerbil's digging stereotypy is a need to hide inside a sheltered space, not a need to dig. The gerbil needs the emotion of

feeling safe, not the action of the digging. (Grandin and Johnson 2010, 4–5)

As both an animal scientist and researcher, Grandin realized and demonstrated how important it is that we "focus on the emotion, not the behavior" in both animals and humans, in all its forms and aspects. Isn't it time we made sure that our classrooms reflect and honour these profound findings?

Sam: At Loose Ends

It was early October, a month into the start of the school year, when Sam suddenly joined our class for adolescents with developmental needs. Sam had only just started attending his new high school after successfully completing Grade 8. But after his first month, he was removed from his Grade 9 special education credit program and placed in my non-credit life skills class. His transition to his new school had not gone smoothly, as old inappropriate behaviours had begun to resurface, behaviours he had overcome when he first began elementary school. He had already demonstrated in his intermediate school that he was responsible, bright, and capable of earning credits at the high school level. The transition team at his intermediate school maintained their support for his placement in a special education Grade 9 credit program, even after being informed of the re-emergence of his troubling behaviour.

Shortly after arriving at high school, Sam began to pull obsessively at loose threads on his shirt or sweater, until almost nothing was left but scraps of material. When this old behaviour resurfaced, the staff took the view that, although Sam was capable, his behaviour was unacceptable; a *non-credit* program, where behavioural rather than academic needs would be the focus, was deemed to be a more appropriate place for addressing these concerns. Sam had not yet had an opportunity to demonstrate his strengths and abilities to his new teachers; instead, his behaviour was all they could see, and his "deficits" rather than his strengths became their primary focus. It was believed that his behaviour must be addressed before learning could begin. Again, the deficits-based model of teaching overshadowed a student's intellectual strengths, to that student's detriment. While problematic behaviours should of course not be ignored, *neither should strengths*. A strength-based approach would address both behaviour *and* learning.

The re-emergence of an old behaviour at a time of great change and transition indicated to me that the behaviour itself was not the problem; rather, it was an expression of Sam's anxiety as he struggled to find a way to cope with his new school and the many overwhelming challenges that went with it. Try as I might, I had great difficulty influencing the decision about Sam's placement in my class, as I advocated for continuation in the Grade 9 credit program along with new strategies and supports to help him cope. The special education consultant who had worked with Sam for many years also advocated for the same, but was informed that high school standards and expectations are much different from what goes on at the elementary and intermediate levels.

When Sam first joined our class, he was highly anxious, as he now had to deal with yet another change. No plan had been put in place to gradually introduce him to his new situation, nor had the class had an opportunity to prepare for our new student. Sam was clearly overwhelmed and frightened. As soon as he joined our class, he began to cry and to pull at a loose thread on his sweatshirt. Who could blame him? After a few days, his crying finally ceased, but he continued to pull at the threads of his sleeve. I did not interfere with his thread pulling, as I could see that he found it calming and that he needed time to adjust to his new classroom and classmates. I had extra T-shirts on hand, just in case.

I explained privately to the class, when Sam was not present, that adjusting to a new school was hard for Sam and he found comfort by pulling at threads. We discussed how people behave when feeling stressed, and shared personal stories.

ON THE ROAD TO INDEPENDENCE

OUR CLASSROOM was set up so students could move freely from one activity station to the next in order for them to have more control over decisions that were matched with their interests and abilities. I believe that by adolescence, students should have more independence and gradually move away from external prompts or direct control by teachers and educational assistants.

Sam's thread-pulling behaviour continued for the first week but then began to decrease, along with his level of anxiety, and he soon developed an interest in our classroom mini-greenhouse. By recognizing the source of Sam's anxiety and redirecting his attention and intellect to classroom activities that might interest him, I was able to make him more comfortable in his new surroundings, so he could begin to relax and would no longer need to pull at threads. With the focus on his strengths and abilities along with more appropriate ways of dealing with anxiety, Sam began to flourish. This was definitely a turning point for him, as he became captivated by our classroom planting project and fascinated with the seeds just beginning to germinate.

There were many learning stations around the room, where students were free to work at their own pace. On his own initiative, Sam began to sketch the daily growth of our plants, complete with measurements and labels. He came up with this idea on his own; it was not one of the activities I had set up. However, his interest in plants was most appropriate for Grade 9 science, so I introduced him to a math and science computer simulations program called Gizmos, which has proven extremely beneficial for students who respond well to lessons online. Sam was captivated by the photosynthesis simulation, which allows students to control and vary the amount of water and sunlight, and then virtually monitor the effect on the plant.

Gizmos are wonderful, dynamic, and interactive math and science simulations used in many schools.

explorelearning.com

As we developed our learning partnership, I followed Sam's lead and encouraged him to become involved with our planting projects. He seemed pleased when I provided him with a copy of our chart showing the life cycle of plants, which I quickly labelled to include the scientific terms he had used with Gizmos (terms like *photosynthesis* and, as I wrote, *chlorophyl*). The very next morning, as soon as Sam got to class, he couldn't wait to inform me that I had misspelled *chlorophyll*. I was both astounded and pleased by his awareness of my mistake and asked him how he came to notice it. He replied that he had gone home and looked it up: "Chlorophyll has two *l*s not one," he said. He had still been thinking about the day's lesson and had done his own research! I praised him for his efforts and quickly added the forgotten *l*. Once again, I was grateful for the guidance and help provided by one of my students. You can be sure that I never made that spelling error again, but I learned a far more valuable lesson that day. Yes, spelling does count—in more ways than I ever imagined.

After a few weeks, the picking of threads had all but disappeared. When I noticed that Sam was feeling anxious, I distracted him by suggesting that he help me shred paper, which I thought might act as a more appropriate substitute for relieving tension. I offered three methods: tear the paper by hand, use scissors to cut it up, or use a small portable shredder. He first went for tearing the paper by hand, but after watching me use the paper shredder, he was fascinated and switched to what he called our confetti-making machine. I told him that whenever he felt anxious, he could simply use the shredder to help him relax. I also introduced him to scrapbooking and cutting pictures from sports magazines, which also seemed to help him relax and gave him great pleasure as he proudly shared his scrapbook with fellow sports fans. Sam was a devoted soccer fan and knew all the players and stats by heart, and his breadth of knowledge impressed many of his classmates.

After a month in our classroom, Sam was happy and more relaxed, and his inappropriate coping strategy had been replaced with more positive ways to relieve his anxiety. His intellectual interests were encouraged, and he could now demonstrate his abilities and true potential. Sadly, though, Sam never returned to the credit program, in spite of my insistence that he was ready and capable. "Best not to rock the boat," I was told, now that he had settled into his routine. Many believed Sam was doing well, and moving him back to his credit program might result in the return of inappropriate behaviour. Why create more problems? But I knew he could do better, and we could have done better by him.

Sam's story shows the importance of placing greater value on abilities and strengths and on our own willingness to take on the challenge of constantly stretching our students and our expectations of what is possible. I believe things are slowly beginning to change—though, unfortunately, not in time for Sam.

But a new business model might just point us in the right direction: with encouragement from a family friend, Sam eventually applied to Specialisterne. He was admitted to this social entrepreneurship organization's training program, and found employment at a bank using his computer skills.

The Specialisterne Foundation harnesses the talents of people with autism and similar challenges, and has created more than a million jobs through "social entrepreneurship, corporate sector engagement, and a global change in mindset." Originally founded in Denmark, Specialisterne now operates in fourteen other countries around the world.

specialisterne.com

Great Expectations: The *dis*Ability Edge

A wonderful demonstration of how our attitudes influence our expectations can be found in the world of work. It is the business world that has taken the lead in discovering the abilities of people who are different.

A *Globe and Mail* article called "Working Wisdom: How Workers with Disabilities Give Companies an Edge" (Grant

2015) highlighted what happens in the workforce when people with "disabilities" are valued because of their strengths and "*dis*Ability edge." I love this term, as it captures the value of viewing people in a positive light when both abilities and disabilities are taken together. The article recognizes the value of a workforce that has been ignored for far too long, powerfully demonstrating what happens when a change in mindset opens up opportunities for people with disabilities who previously were not considered an asset and might have been given a job only as an act of kindness rather than because it was a good business decision. Here, the hiring is based not on charity but on good business sense. In the article, Garth Johnson, co-founder of Meticulon Consulting Inc., a Calgary-based technology firm, said, "I'm not interested in this as a charity. If we can't prove business value, then I don't view it as sustainable for our employees, either our typically enabled or our people with autism. Business will bail on it as soon as it's not bringing in real returns."

The article, which appeared in the business section rather than the life section, sends an important message to businesses and employers: "[E]mployers have found that disabled employees have unique abilities and tend to work harder to prove themselves. Turnover rates and absenteeism are also often lower." Companies and organizations like Specialisterne, Google, Microsoft, Walgreen, Toronto Dominion Bank, Tim Hortons, and Good Foot Delivery (goodfootdelivery.com)— a nonprofit courier service in Toronto—have all discovered what is possible when deserving people are given a chance.

ON MARCH 10, 2017, TVO (TV Ontario) aired an excellent documentary called *Autism Grows Up*. The show follows six Canadian adults with ASD in their search for meaningful work. Included in the documentary is a wonderful interview with Temple Grandin. You can view *Autism Grows Up* on YouTube at youtube.com/watch?v=gRl_k6gHW_4. Also at TVO is the documentary series *Employable Me*, which can be seen at tvo.org/programs/employable-me.

Tally: The Knitting Lesson

Another student of mine also had a tendency to obsessively pull at threads or scratch her skin until it was raw and sore. Tally, a quiet girl of fifteen, kept to herself and rarely initiated conversation.

Around the time Tally joined our class, a few teachers and some parent volunteers with a passion for knitting decided to start a knitting club at lunchtime. Such activities were not part of the school's program, with its focus on more behavioural concerns; art activities, handicrafts, and music were often dependent on the particular interests and generosity of such volunteers. In other words, these programs were provided more by chance than by design, yet so many students benefitted from them.

Tally was intrigued, and we both decided to join. She caught on right away and quickly surpassed me and many of the other students with her natural talent. We were all impressed with her innate ability and her prolific production of fashionable hats and scarves. She was soon selling her crafts and taking orders from many staff members. She started to come out of her shell and seemed more comfortable talking to people, especially if it was about knitting. Tally was proud of her newly discovered talent and seemed to enjoy the attention. She wore her knitted Harry Potter scarf with her newfound confidence as a tribute to one of her favourite books. The entire class had recently discovered Harry Potter, and everyone admired Tally's handiwork.

I suggested Tally keep her knitting close at hand, and that when she felt anxious in class, she could pick it up to help her relax. The feel of the wool seemed to offer Tally a great sense of comfort, whether through the knitting process itself or pulling at the wool to correct mistakes; but it was her new sense of self and pride in her work that was most transformative. Her old, inappropriate behaviours now found positive expression in colourful scarves with matching caps and a new sense of wonder. Previously, she had spoken only when spoken to; now she began to initiate conversations about knitting. She also loved helping others with their knitting projects—especially me, for I kept mysteriously dropping stitches, no matter how hard I tried.

Tally flourished when she discovered her passion for knitting and a more meaningful connection to the world around her. She and my other students taught me that when we stay open to new experiences and a different way of viewing unique minds, we can focus on what is really important and valuable—the strengths and talents of our students. And very soon, the strengths begin to get stronger and the weaknesses begin to fade from view.

I must confess that I was amazed by the results of this "knitting lesson," which had taught me far more than how to knit and purl. The experience helped me gain a deeper understanding of what lies beneath behaviours and how the feelings, thoughts, and anxieties expressed through certain behaviours are not much different from the things we *all* feel and experience. Whether we bite our nails, pick at our cuticles, scratch our skin, flap our hands, or pull at threads, the underlying feelings are much the same; how we learn to cope with overwhelming feelings is the issue. If we can redirect inappropriate behaviours by first accepting and understanding them, the chances of a successful outcome will increase. If pulling at a thread obsessively can be redirected into a knitting activity or using a paper shredder, then suddenly a problematic behaviour can be turned into a strength and even an opportunity—to work in a knitting shop, sell handiwork, or work in an office shredding paper, delivering mail, photocopying—or simply to discover a new passion and the pure joy it offers.

THE EALING SCHOOL
A STITCH IN TIME SAVES NINE

IT WAS only during the course of writing this book that I discovered the work of gifted teacher Sybil Elgar. In the 1960s, Elgar was hired to teach at the first school for autistic children in London; she was trained in the Montessori method and successfully incorporated many of its materials and techniques in her classroom. Elgar and Lorna Wing partnered to write a practical and concise teaching booklet, which said, "If they are unoccupied, autistic children tend to harm themselves through biting, head banging, picking at sore places, or scratching their faces and arms. This tendency is made much worse by the wrong kind of institutional life. This tragic outcome can be avoided by providing individual attention in a stimulating and *educating* environment. This is what we try to do at Ealing" (1969, 28). The program at the Ealing School therefore included the teaching of "handwork" (22–23): "A handwork programme must cover a wide range of ability. It is necessary to begin with simple work with bead threading, paper cutting, and scissor and glue work. After that some children can progress to collage and simple sewing patterns, and later to weaving, basketry, toy making, embroidery, making models, lino cutting, making and decorating lamp shades, making jewellery, cutting and shaping of copper, and enamelling. Autistic children do not learn these skills quickly or easily; indeed work requiring a variety of slow processes before completion appeals to the more adjusted and stable among the group."

Sybil Elgar was greatly influenced by Montessori's recognition of the importance of tactile and sensory learning experiences as an integral part of child development, especially for children facing developmental challenges.

MARIA MONTESSORI

IN 1896, a young woman named Maria Montessori had the honour and distinction of being the first female in Italy to receive a doctor of medicine degree. More importantly, she would become an advocate and champion for the many long-forgotten "feebleminded" children locked away in insane asylums.

Shortly after assuming her first medical position as an assistant at the University of Rome's psychiatric clinic, Montessori would encounter a group of children who would capture both her heart and her mind, and who would impact the lives of countless generations thereafter. It was a day she would never forget. She was carrying out her new duties, which included making daily rounds in the asylum, when she came across a group of unhappy children huddled together in a room that resembled a prison cell. The children were confined to the care of a miserable woman who looked down on her wards with disgust. Montessori asked the woman to explain her feelings of contempt toward these unfortunate children, and the woman replied, "As soon as their meals are finished they throw themselves on the floor to search for crumbs" (Standing 1962, 28). Montessori looked around the room and immediately saw that it was absolutely bare: no toys to play with, nothing for the children to hold or explore with their fingers—except, of course, for the crumbs they managed to find on the floor.

It was at this moment, according to Montessori's biographer, E.M. Standing, that "she saw these poor creatures and their environment with an eye illuminated by the light of genius" (28). She was alarmed by the prison-like treatment of the children and began searching for a way to help them. She spent as much time as possible with the children and soon came to realize that their "mental deficiency was a pedagogical problem rather than a medical one." She believed that these children did not need to be locked away in hospital wards as if they were ill, but instead should be placed in schools where their deficiencies could be addressed and abilities and skills could be developed through hands-on experience and special education treatment. I hate to imagine what might have happened if Montessori had simply continued on her rounds, stepping over the crumbs, past the children, never looking back.

Influenced by the work of French doctors Jean Itard and Édouard Séguin, Montessori continued to develop her emerging pedagogical philosophy. Her work came to the attention of the Italian minister of education, who decided to create a state school under her direction. Students in Rome who were considered to be "hopelessly deficient" were the first to be enrolled, followed later by "all the idiot children from the insane asylums in Rome" (Standing 1962, 29).[1] Before too long, the children in her new school began to flourish, far exceeding what many believed was possible.

Montessori spent much of her time developing her program and training teachers "in a special method of observation and in the education of feebleminded children" (29). She quickly recognized the important role a well-trained teacher could play in improving the lives of these children, and decided to join the teachers in order to learn first-hand how best to help them. This would now become her full-time job—teaching during the day and working into the wee hours to reflect, analyze, and develop new materials. She also came to realize that the special education methods she was developing were simply based on sound educational principles, "more rational than those in general use."

So successful were her methods that some children from the asylums learned to read and write, and many even passed the public examinations for "normal" children. Her comments about this remarkable result are quite telling (Standing 1962, 29–30): "Whilst everyone was admiring my idiots I was searching for the reasons which could keep back the healthy and happy children of the ordinary schools on so low a plane that they could be equaled in tests of intelligence by my unfortunate pupils… I became convinced that similar methods applied to normal children would develop and set free their personality in a marvelous and surprising way."

Montessori and all of her students were profoundly impacted by their shared, life-changing educational experience, and she came to realize that the "form of creation which was necessary for these unfortunate beings, so as to enable them to reenter society, to take their place in the civilized world and render them independent of the help of others—placing human dignity within their grasp—was a work which appealed so strongly to my heart that I remained in it for years" (29–30). And so Montessori continued her search for excellent teaching methods for *all* children in order to realize everyone's full potential.

Due to the great success of what came to be known as the Montessori Method, schools for typical and gifted children soon opened up around the world, giving many more children the opportunity to benefit from this well-developed, hands-on sensory approach to learning. Recently, there has been a renewed interest in using the Montessori Method for children with autism. Montessori's legacy continues to thrive, beautifully demonstrating that her special education methods represent teaching at its best, with advantages for all students.

MONTESSORI (1912) 1964 Standing 1962

2

When Words Fail, There's Poetry

WHEN I FIRST began working with adolescent students with autisitic tendencies and developmental differences, I was surprised to discover that while some of them could read quite well, others were not able to read or write except for some basic functional words. Regardless of reading level, it appeared that my students' previous educational programs had offered little exposure to the wonderful world of books. Reviewing their school records, I could see that their early years had been focused mainly on their deficits and on changing their behaviours; their educational needs seemed to be less of a priority and were only developed as far as was considered necessary. Once the students entered high school, teachers like me were encouraged to maintain and reinforce skills and abilities already learned, rather than introducing new skills, "rocking the boat," or stretching students beyond what was comfortable and familiar.

Many professionals believed that if students hadn't learned to read by the time they entered high school, then it was too late to start, particularly in light of their learning challenges and more pressing behavioural concerns. In fact, many still believe that introducing new challenges might raise false hope and result in disappointment, and that the window of opportunity for addressing a child's needs exists only during the early years. (Doesn't this sound a lot like the early misconceptions about learning disabled adolescents?)

Discovering new interests and abilities during adolescence was not considered a priority. But what if many of the students had never actually been taught how to read beyond the functional level? Wasn't it worth trying?

The research clearly shows that adolescence offers another critical period for further learning and development. Lorna Wing observed this back in 1972, in reference to a study of sixty-three adolescents and young adults with autism. She concluded (150–51), "The workers carrying out this study noted that improvement in learning and the acquisition of skills often continued into adult life. They pointed out that although to be most successful education should begin early, no age can be said to be 'too late' to begin teaching an autistic child. The study also emphasized the importance of providing suitable facilities for further education and training for employment after leaving school." We shouldn't let this critical stage in development go to waste. Instead, we should double our efforts to take full advantage of this important opportunity to stretch our students toward achieving new goals. Gaps in their education can be addressed and new interests and abilities can be introduced and developed.

I was initially discouraged by other educators and professionals from teaching my adolescent students how to read beyond the functional level and was told that more relevant and practical programming concerns should be the immediate focus. Books, literature, poetry, and drama were considered irrelevant and unimportant in the lives of children with special needs, and our primary focus should be to continue to address their behaviour and life/social skills. I agreed, but didn't see why I couldn't do both. In fact, I discovered that a more multifaceted approach enhanced my students' social skills while simultaneously opening up the world of books, ideas, and new interests and passions.

Relying on my experience teaching learning disabled adolescents how to read, I ignored the deficits-based curriculum model and instead persisted with a strength-based model. As a result, many of my students improved their reading and writing skills, and developed a love of reading and a lifelong connection with the public library, a place where new interests could be explored. Role-playing, drama skits, puppet shows, dioramas, and library outings brought literature to life for the students. It was obvious to me that improved communication and literacy skills help naturally develop a sense of connection, and I did see an improvement in their social skills. Beautifully written stories capture the human spirit and offer important life lessons.

Since most of my students had recieved limited exposure to literature or poetry in elementary/middle school, I realized we would need to fill in those gaps. Deciding which books to choose was a challenge that my students and I fully embraced. So many wonderful books—where to begin?

We spent one afternoon a week at the local library, where I made sure every one of my students had their own library card. The students couldn't believe that they didn't need money to borrow a book, and said that was "cool" or gave me the thumbs-up. A whole new world of books opened up for them, and their local library would become a wonderful resource and meaningful connection to their community for years to come. Their personal education could continue, even after their formal public education came to an end at the age of twenty-one.

Eric: The Heart of a Poet

We began to discover the wonderful world of books, including the Harry Potter series, which was all the rage at that time, and also to develop an interest in poetry.

One student soon became our classroom's resident poet, a much-deserved honour. Eric's fascination with words had been evident from an early age. His precocious reading ability had also played a critical role in his language development. Eric enjoyed writing poetry and seemed most comfortable expressing his true feelings through the poetic form. This allowed for greater artistic freedom of expression, beyond the confines and rules of prosaic conventions.

With Eric as their role model, and inspired by his enthusiasm and encouragement, the other students quickly followed his lead and tried their hand at composing poems. On one of our weekly visits to the library, we discovered *Young Voices*, the Toronto Public Library's magazine featuring peer-selected teen writing, poetry, and artwork by high school students from across the city. It was considered a great achievement and honour to have work selected for the popular publication, which had a circulation of more than 18,000. How cool, we thought, to celebrate and enjoy the creative efforts of fellow students. *Young Voices* became a real class favourite.

I decided to submit one of Eric's poems to the magazine, and we were thrilled when it was selected for publication. When the poem was published, Eric was recognized at a public ceremony, and this momentous honour was not lost on him or his family. The audience's overwhelming acceptance of Eric and the artistic honesty behind his words made his poetry even more meaningful. Oh, the joy of finally being heard and understood by so many people.

Rose, Where Did You Get That Red?

By Eric Lewin

magic spells could
    say make it work
paint it yellow orange
    green pink red
we need paint brushes with
    long brown handles
we need brushes and paint cans
we need to open the cans
mix the paint
swimming oceans of red
we need long brushes
we need paint to make it pink
we need 60 paint brushes and
    long strokes of red on the rose
the rose is marvelous
the rose is exquisite
the rose is perfect

Kenneth Koch's *Rose, Where Did You Get That Red?* is an excellent book for teaching poetry to children. Eric used the title of the book for his poem.

REPRINTED FROM SHELF LIFE

Toronto Library News and Views (Kernohan 2008)

Poetic Injustice

Poetry became a popular form of self-expression for all of my students. They particularly enjoyed writing acrostic poems, shape poems, or poems that began with a question I provided. Their poetry was displayed on our classroom bulletin board for all to see and enjoy.

One day we were visited by a special education professional interested in learning about programs for adolescent learners. We proudly presented our collection of student poetry, now beautifully bound in a laminated book. But I wasn't quite prepared for this educator's response after she had leafed through the pages. She turned to me and asked, "Do your students even know what their poems mean?" I realized in this moment that there was nothing more I could say. The poems said it all, yet sadly this educator could not see into the hearts of true poets.

As often happens, I eventually thought of a response to this educator long after she walked away from our classroom. I had found myself at a loss for words, but the philosopher John Stuart Mill knew just what to say. I wish I had remembered his description of poetry at the time:

> It has often been asked, What is Poetry?... the word "poetry" imports something quite peculiar in its nature... something which does not even require the instrument of words, but can speak through the other audible symbols called musical sounds, and even through the visible ones which are the language of sculpture, painting, and architecture—all this, we believe, is and must be felt, though perhaps indistinctly, by all upon whom poetry in any of its shapes produces an impression beyond that of tickling the ear. (1860, 93)

Music, poetry, and any other artistic expression—whether it is a Lego sculpture, a knitted scarf, a cultivated garden, origami chess pieces, a perfectly executed freehand drawing to scale of the dashboard of a student's family car (from memory), or designing humane livestock-handling facilities all over the world—all represent the essence of poetry and our connection to others.

What Is Literacy?

In their book *A Land We Can Share: Teaching Literacy to Students with Autism* (2008), Paula Kluth and Kelly Chandler-Olcott, at Syracuse University, recognize how transforming an enriched classroom experience can be for children on the spectrum. As experts in the field of education, they address the critical need to teach literacy to students with autism, which has been sadly overlooked in a curriculum of functional life skills. They document the success and progress of students who are exposed to enriched literacy experiences:

> [R]esearchers in the past few years have begun to explore a broader range of issues related to how students with autism learn to read and write, with these investigations often set in richer and more authentic contexts than was previously the case. Rita Colasent and Penny Griffith (1998) published one of the first studies of this kind to come to our attention... Before the study, these students had been exposed only to a curriculum of functional life skills... Yet they bloomed when given opportunities to listen and discuss stories on the same theme, with all of them demonstrating the ability to "state a title, state their favorite character, and describe their personal feelings" after listening to the target texts (1998, 416)... Despite the fact that these students had received no reading instruction before the study began—their individualized education programs included no reading goals and labeled them as "essentially non-readers" (Colasent & Griffith, 1998, 415)—they had clearly developed some important skills related to literacy that no one noticed or valued prior to the project. They were able to develop these skills as a result of lessons that we would not classify as "special" interventions or strategies; instead,

they were given opportunities to engage in literacy activities common in many general education classrooms. (28)

A Land We Can Share: Teaching Literacy to Students with Autism, by Paula Kluth and Kelly Chandler-Olcott, should be required reading for all educators and parents.

On Reading, by Ken Goodman, offers helpful insights and techniques that I have used with many of my students with dyslexia.

Beginning to Read, by Marilyn Jager Adams, is an excellent resource for how best to teach children how to read. (Summary version also available.)

Sarah Ward Cognitive Connections provides an excellent set of tools for developing executive function and comprehension skills.

efpractice.com

The authors (2008, 28–29) go on to ask the questions I had also asked when I first met my students and realized they had little previous exposure to books: "How had these students' abilities and skills been overlooked prior to the study? Why did their diagnosis of autism construct them as 'non-readers' who were therefore unable to benefit from literacy instruction? What might they have been able to do if provided with a steady diet of rich literacy experiences, not just a 2-week intervention?"

In their attempt to understand the issues raised by their questions, Kluth and Chandler-Olcott, like Temple Grandin, recognize the role the deficits-based model has played in setting up barriers to educational opportunities: "[F]or students with autism labels... the 'medical model' understanding of such a label can erode the basic optimism that many educators have about children's potential. The lack of that optimism generally translates into a lack of expectation and opportunity that becomes a self-fulfilling prophecy" (33).

PAULA KLUTH AND WILLIAM CRUIKSHANK

PAULA KLUTH is probably both the best and best known "go-to" teacher for autism spectrum disorder. She is popular with both parents and teachers, bringing a wealth of experience from the field of education—she is a former special educator, an inclusion facilitator, classroom teacher at both the elementary and secondary school level, professor, researcher, and author. Kluth is also a much sought-after speaker and a regular presenter at the International Geneva Centre Autism conference in Toronto. On her website (paulakluth.com), you can learn about the latest classroom ideas, lessons, webinars, or resources, or sign up for her newsletter.

During her tenure as an assistant professor in the Department of Teaching and Leadership at Syracuse University, Kluth focused much of her research on determining how to achieve the best learning outcomes for public school students with ASD and developmental needs. Her ongoing work in this area challenges educators to examine current practices that may limit educational opportunities for students of all ages and abilities. Her books demonstrate the importance of moving away from the deficits-based special education model, which still maintains a tight hold on the way these students are often perceived, presenting instead a strength-based approach to learning and skill development based on a more neurological understanding of "learning and mislearning." This idea of the neurological nature of learning for students with special needs was first advocated by William Cruikshank, who was the first to envision special education as a distinct discipline, and established the Department of Education for Exceptional Children in Syracuse University's School of Education in 1946.

Cruikshank was committed to improving the lives of all children with exceptionalities, both intellectual and physical. He was especially interested in overcoming many of the misunderstandings associated with "learning disabilities," which was a relatively new concept in the 1960s. His efforts eventually paid off, as he demonstrated that special education pedagogy is simply teaching at its best. His approach to and understanding of "learning and mislearning" was so successful that it would eventually become the basis for differentiated instruction and universal design, now standard practice in many public schools. Just as Montessori demonstrated the value of special education pedagogy for all students, so too did Cruikshank appreciate that a neurologically informed approach to teaching would benefit all learners.

One of Kluth's favourite sayings is, "Dwell in possibility." Perhaps if the lessons from the past are finally allowed to inform the lessons of the future, educators will welcome the opportunity to make a meaningful difference in the lives of so many deserving students.

KLUTH N.D. Kluth and Chandler-Olcott 2008

The Fine Art of Teaching

Art became an important part of our classroom routine, not in the therapeutic sense in which it is often seen in the context of special education, but simply as another interest or passion to explore or celebrate, in the same way as it is experienced by students in mainstream programs. Art is even more vital for students with special needs—yet these activities are often considered optional rather than a necessary aspect of their education.

Corking, beadwork, loom work, boondoggle, jewellery making, clay work, and painting offer enjoyable opportunities to discover new talents and make new friends with similar interests, while providing a reason to communicate with others and share their passion. Art is communication at the most personal level, often surpassing the boundaries of the spoken word. For individuals with language challenges, art also offers a different opportunity to communicate and connect.

I remember with fondness a very gifted teacher who also happened to be a talented professional musician. On her own initiative, she developed an enriched music program for students with special needs. She volunteered to work with students every day during the lunch hour and, like the Pied Piper, was soon surrounded by eager students who quickly ate their lunches in order to join the group of budding musicians and singers. "Miss T" relied on friends and family to support her initiative, through donated instruments, performances by visiting musicians, and raising funds to purchase choir shirts, proudly worn by the students when performing at seniors' homes and festivals. Miss T did it all—and the students often shouted "Bravo!"—literally—to express appreciation for their beloved teacher.

Through Miss T's dedication and generosity of spirit, parents and teachers suddenly became aware of the passion and talent that had been hiding within our students. Beautiful singers, drummers with a soulful heartbeat, and inspired improvisational dancers came to life on the stage—but most impressive of all was the students' discovery of a previously unrealized gift for music within themselves, along with a more meaningful way to form close connections with others. Pride could be seen on their faces as they performed and brought joy to their audience, especially when performing at homes for the elderly. How wonderful to be able to give back to others instead of always receiving—to really become a contributing member of the community. These fortunate opportunities are offered more by chance than by design, though, as artistic endeavours seem to fall outside of regular programming considerations for children who are different. Even in mainstream programs, there have been massive cuts to arts education.

VIVA SINGERS
WHERE EACH VOICE MATTERS

IN 2000, recently retired high school music teacher Carol Woodward Ratzlaff founded the VIVA! Youth Singers of Toronto (vivayouthsingers.com) in response to widespread cuts to school art programs. The many choirs that make up VIVA! include singers and musicians of all ages, and abilities, at both the amateur and professional levels. The organization's tagline is "Where Each Voice Matters," in recognition of its inclusive and welcoming philosophy.

To that end, several VIVA staff members visited L'Arche in France, one of the first communities for people with disabilities. It is now part of an international network providing both residential and vocational support. Members play an active role contributing to life in their neighbourhood and are encouraged to pursue personal goals and interests.

Several of my former students are enthusiastic members of this choir. A few years ago, when a video was being made about VIVA!'s vision of inclusion, one of my students was asked if he'd like to be in the video. He declined, so he was asked instead what was most important to him about VIVA! "The audience," he replied.

I was told this story in an email I received from a parent. In it, she added, "I just love that. Imagine, a person with autism, the stereotype of which is impairment in social skills and communication—but his comment indicates the very opposite—he very clearly wants to reach out and communicate."

When I asked to have art added to our timetable, I was turned down. I was told that an art therapist was scheduled to visit our class the following term (for only one hour per week for six weeks), so there was no need and I should wait. I explained that I simply wanted an art class and some supplies available to my students on a regular basis; our interest was in pursuing art activities, not therapy per se. Not willing to take no for an answer, I found some free surplus art materials online (donated by other teachers) and made art an "unofficial" part of our daily routine. I arranged for artists to volunteer in our class, helping out and teaching us their craft. Many of my students discovered previously hidden artistic abilities and talents, and we even arranged an art show at the end of the term for all to enjoy—a real success. I tried to provide a classroom environment where discoveries could be made, passions realized, and interests and talents nourished.

The Creative Growth Art Center in Oakland, California, is the oldest and largest nonprofit art studio for people with developmental, intellectual, and physical disabilities.

creativegrowth.org

New York City's Strokes of Genius, founded by Rosa C. Martinez, celebrates and helps develop the artistic abilities of individuals on the spectrum.

trainthetalent.net

3

Too Much of a Good Thing

CHILDREN ON THE spectrum are encouraged from an early age to follow written/icon schedules to allow for easy transitions. I completely agree with this strategy—when it works, it's great. But when life's unpredictable events interfere and disrupt our plans, disaster and meltdowns often follow. Working with schedules and learning how to adapt when things change will help students develop transition skills as they navigate the detours of daily life.

Ellen: It's about Time (aka Lesson 1)

Ellen was very good at following clear instructions and schedules. She remembered everyone's birthday. Her father affectionately referred to her as his personal assistant and "human Blackberry," regularly reminding him about his upcoming dental appointments, hockey games, wedding anniversaries, and other important events—for which he was most grateful.

Ellen loved schedules. Schedules make a chaotic and unpredictable world more manageable and provide a sense of control. But of course it is just that, a *sense* of control, as real control is not possible. So what can we do to prepare our students for days that don't run like clockwork?

One day, after visiting her eye doctor, Ellen handed me a note indicating that she needed to be given eye drops every day at noon for the next two weeks. The eye drops were kept in the main office and would be administered by one of the educational assistants at lunchtime.

The next day, as our class got ready for lunch, the noon bell rang and Ellen immediately began to pace. She started to panic and screamed, "It is twelve o'clock—eye drops—the doctor said!" Then she began to repeat the doctor's instructions, "Ellen must have eye drops at noon..." Unfortunately, the educational assistant was delivering medications to other students and hadn't yet arrived. I called the office to get the assistant to come directly to our class, as nothing else would calm Ellen. When she finally received her drops, she settled down but was completely worn out for the rest of the day.

This was not the first time that a change or delay in a schedule had resulted in a student having a meltdown. The recovery and the effect on the student and other members of the class could disrupt the entire school day and have a negative impact on the learning environment in the classroom.

I realized that for Ellen, noon meant 12:00 sharp. She remembered the doctor's exact words and, with her tendency to rely on the literal, took the word "must" at face value, believing that something catastrophic might happen if the doctor's exact instructions were not followed.

Literal and exact interpretations of what many of my students heard throughout the day often resulted in a very black and white view of the world—the doctor had said "noon" and noon it must be. The schedules they had been taught to follow and rely on from their early years had become a fixed and rigid strategy in their daily lives, one that created a sense of order and predictability. This made them feel safe and prepared, and helped them manage their day. Schedules also serve as a helpful tool for educators and provide structure and a means to prepare students for what lies ahead. Unfortunately, life doesn't always work that way. An overreliance on schedules without built-in wiggle room to accommodate the unpredictable, as many of us know, can lead to meltdowns.

I definitely needed to figure this out. How could I work with schedules, a proven and effective strategy, while at the same time developing my students' ability to be more flexible when things didn't go according to plan?

The next day, long before noon, I sat the class down for a lesson on time. Now, everyone in the class was an expert on time; I mean, even without a clock in sight, my students had an uncanny ability to know exactly what time it was. It was quite remarkable. So why the lesson on time? Well, I realized that there was still one lesson they hadn't been taught: *ish*. Why had it taken me so long to figure this out?

So, I gathered the class around and began our lesson.

"Okay, everyone, today we are going to learn about time. Now, I know you are very good at telling time and following schedules. You are the best. So let's do some review."

Holding up both a digital and an analog clock, I pointed to 11:15 and asked, "What time is it?"

"Kenny, yes, it is 11:15."

"Tally, please turn the hands of the clock to show 11:30," I continued. "Perfect."

"Sam, please change the clock to 11:45 ... Thank you."

"Ellen, please show us 12 o'clock ... Wonderful."

Pause.

"Now, class, who can show us 12-*ish*?"

The class went silent, and then everyone started saying, "*Ish*, 12-*ish*" over and over again, giggling with delight at the funny sound and silly time.

"Well," I continued, "we all know time markers like o'clock, thirty, half past, noon, and others—but my favourite time marker is *ish*. Where is it on the clock? Let's figure it out together…"

I continued, "Let's look at 12 o'clock. When the clock indicates exactly 12, we can say it is 12 'on the dot' [pause] *or* we can say it is 12 sharp [pause] *or* we can say it's noon [pause] *or*—[Ellen raises her hand] yes, Ellen, that's right, we can also say 12 o'clock." [long pause]

"So, I wonder, does anyone know where 12-*ish* is on the clock? [pause] Can anyone show us?" Giggles, but no volunteers.

"Twelve-*ish* can be a little before 12 or a little after 12. It is *not* 'on the dot'—it is 'off the dot.'" I demonstrated *ish* at several different places on the clock. "It can be a little bit before *or* a little bit after. It falls in the *ish* zone."

I continued: "Today, Ellen will have her eye drops around 12 o'clock, or 12-*ish* or noon-*ish*. [pause] Unless we are told 'on the dot,' any time can be in the *ish* zone."

Again, the class spontaneously began to chant and laugh, "Noon-*ish*, *ish*, *ish*, noon-*ish*!"

"So, let's practice: The school bus will be here at 4 o'clock, but it is raining so it might be a little bit after 4 o'clock or around 4 o'clock. What time will the bus arrive?"

I prompted the class with a hand gesture, and they responded loudly, "4-*ish*," still giggling at the this funny *ish* ending.

For the rest of the week, they adopted *ish* for every hour of our day. They loved the sound, and the fact that even when "trains, planes, and automobiles" don't run on time, there is always *ish* and no more need to panic. We had discovered the "*ish* zone" and its rightful place on our schedules.

From that day forward, whenever a student became anxious about things not going according to schedule, I simply reminded them of *ish* and all was well.

As for Ellen, she enjoyed following schedules and making lists, so she was a natural when it came to accurately following recipes. She also enjoyed cooking and baking and was hired by Lemon & Allspice (commongroundco-op.ca/about-lemon-and-allspice), a catering business that uses a co-operative business model, where employees with special needs share in the company's profits. Developing Ellen's strengths led to enjoyable work and a sense of satisfaction.

ERIC SCHOPLER AND GARY MESIBOV

IN 1965, when Lorna Wing and the National Society for Autistic Children (now the National Autistic Society) established the first school for autistic children (now the Sybil Elgar School), one of its first visitors was Eric Schopler, a professor of psychiatry and psychology at the University of North Carolina-Chapel Hill and soon to become the founding director of Treatment and Education of Autistic and Communication related handicapped Children (TEACCH). Schopler was greatly influenced by what he saw at the school, and many of Sybil Elgar's ideas (based on this gifted teacher's Montessori training and background in learning disabilities) would be incorporated into the TEACCH approach/curriculum.

Once back home in North Carolina, Schopler set about putting his ideas into action. He received a research grant that helped lay the foundation for what would become the TEACCH program, the first statewide system for assisting and supporting children with autism and their families. Schopler took a different approach from the Sybil Elgar School when he noted "that one of the key differences was the decision to embed their program in the university, so as to ensure practice reflected empirical research" (Feinstein 2010, 89). Lorna Wing followed Schopler's research with great interest and included one of his papers, "Towards Reducing Behavior Problems in Autistic Children," in the second edition of *Early Childhood Autism* ([1976] 1980).

Schopler's view of behaviour and education is significant and worth restating as we continue to have to advocate for the educational needs of individuals on the spectrum: "Behavior problems, however, have the same basis in the child's perceptual deficits, his language impairment and handicap of understanding, as his special problems of learning" (221). This understanding of behaviour recognized that the school environment could provide the perfect opportunity for addressing many of the child's needs, where meaningful skills could be developed, strengths encouraged, hidden abilities discovered, and relationships formed all within a nurturing social/community setting.

The newly established TEACCH program took the idea of education even further by rejecting the commonly used autism treatments, with their focus on remediating deficits and achieving "normal" behaviour. Instead, Schopler focused on working with the students' differences, nurturing individual strengths and interests while still being mindful of their needs.

The TEACCH curriculum would cultivate a culture of understanding autism by developing meaningful communication skills, encouraging social and leisure interests, and promoting a sense of well-being. The TEACCH approach has been broadened and adapted over the years and is appropriate for all ages and settings, including schools, homes, stores, businesses, camps, recreational settings and programs, job sites, residential programs, post-secondary institutions, and so on.

Schopler was also influenced by Bernard Rimland's neural theory of behaviour, which strongly rejected Bruno Bettelheim's "refrigerator mother"[1] explanation for autism. Schopler and Rimland shared similar views and worked together to help establish the Autism Society of America, following the British example. Schopler not only maintained a productive collaboration with his British colleagues, Lorna Wing and Michael Rutter, one of the founders of the field of child psychiatry in the UK, he also formed an international network of parents and professionals in Canada, Switzerland, Greece, Netherlands, Belgium, France, Italy, South America, Sweden, China, Japan, and, more recently, Nigeria. Closer to home, a collaboration with the North Carolina Department of Public Instruction was established to provide consultation and training with public school classroom teachers and assistants affiliated with TEACCH.

By 1978, as the children in TEACCH were approaching adolescence, Schopler persuaded Gary Mesibov, a professor of psychology at the University of North Carolina, to join TEACCH and spearhead a project directed at providing services for adolescents and adults. The parents and professionals of TEACCH had come to realize that many adolescents and adults with autism would greatly benefit from continuing to receive assistance in pursuing their educational and vocational goals and residential needs. Mesibov developed a successful, internationally recognized adolescent/adult program that included social skills groups, supported employment, and in-service training. Mesibov and Schopler also worked together on a fifteen-year project co-authoring and co-editing a series of books covering the latest topics in autism research while adapting and modifying their eclectic TEACCH approach to match the ongoing research. Due to their efforts, countless individuals around the world have benefitted from the TEACCH approach to autism spectrum disorders.

In 2010, Mesibov was asked by Adam Feinstein, editor of *Looking Up: The Monthly International Autism Magazine* and, later, the author of *A History of Autism: Conversations with the Pioneers* (2010), how he envisioned the future of autism and the field of education. Mesibov responded:

> I think that genetic, brain and pharmacological research will continue to be helpful for autism spectrum disorders, but I am afraid most of these will not translate into the kind of immediate treatment gains or "cures" which many consumers are hoping for and scientists are suggesting. As a result, I am afraid that the hope and promise of scientific and biological interventions will continue to proliferate and dominate a lot of time and energy of many in the field that should be devoted to more promising and empirically validated approaches. (295–96)

Mesibov told Feinstein he was concerned that the educational interventions and work with older individuals that had demonstrated the important advances gained in the field of education continue to remain a low priority, in spite of their success. "Because these techniques are perceived as too slow in producing desired outcomes and do not offer the same promise of achieving hoped-for cures, they will continue to be second-class citizens in our field," he said. "I hope that I am wrong..."

Mesibov retired in 2010, but he has not slowed down or given up his commitment to serving the needs of individuals on the spectrum. You can now find him in his continuing role as a TEACCH ambassador, instructing the intensive three-day TEACCH training course for various organizations around the world. He is especially popular in the UK and is a frequent workshop leader for the National Autistic Society. Mesibov continues to promote the needs of the adolescent/adult learner, and in recent interviews he has highlighted important research conducted by Catherine Johnson that recognizes adolescence as offering yet another important critical developmental stage of intervention for learning new skills, developing abilities, and discovering new talents.

AUTISM UK INDEPENDENT. N.D. Donvan and Zucker 2016; Feinstein 2010; Mesibov, Shea, and Schopler 2004; J. Wing (1966) 1969

A MORE FLEXIBLE WAY OF
DEALING WITH THE WORLD

IN AN interview in 2001, Adam Feinstein asked Gary Mesibov how TEACCH applies the latest findings about the "second intervention window":

> I don't think we ever thought about it from a neurological perspective, but one thing has changed in the way we work with people with autism. We have always had this basic structured teaching strategy philosophy—trying to teach them to use and capitalise on their skills. I can't really say it's because of the neurological findings, but one of the things we started to notice in our adult programs is that there almost needed to be a second level of structured teaching. Children not only needed to learn to use schedules but to be more flexible within those schedules. We found that, sometimes, the children were just memorising schedules. So if there were no chicken fingers for lunch on Friday, for example, a child would have a tantrum. That really should not happen if our system is being used right, because the child should not memorise the schedule but rather be able to look at it each day and change it. They should have a more flexible way of dealing with the world, using the schedule. We are really focusing now on schedules and systems featuring more meaningful skills. The neurological findings suggest that these children should be capable of this, because they are making cognitive advances and expanding.

Angel: It's *Not* about Time (aka Lesson 2)

I still had much to learn about my own automatic habit of reinforcing schedules—as I discovered one day when I failed to listen to a student's true needs.

It was a few minutes before lunchtime and the students were clearing their desks when Angel, a quiet fourteen-year-old girl with limited capacity to express herself in words, suddenly became quite anxious, repeating, with growing intensity, "12 o'clock... 12 o'clock... 12 o'clock!" Without much thought, I fell into the old "reinforce the schedule" strategy, replying, "Yes, Angel, you will have lunch at 12 o'clock." But instead of calming her, my reassurance about the schedule seemed only to agitate her even more. She again repeated the time and I again said yes, it will be lunchtime; this caused her to jump up from her desk and begin to pace back and forth.

What was going on? I was reinforcing the schedule, yet that seemed to make things worse. With her limited ability to express herself, Angel was unable to tell me what was wrong, and I couldn't seem to figure it out. Angel was rarely upset, yet she continued to pace and repeat "12 o'clock" over and over. Finally, she marched over to me in frustration and kicked my chair, and it was at that moment, as I looked in her eyes, that I saw fear, not anger. I now realized that she was afraid of 12 o'clock, so, without thinking, I said, "Would you like to have lunch with me in the classroom today?" Angel immediately relaxed, smiled, said yes, and calmly sat down at her desk. I now understood that Angel was afraid of something happening at lunchtime, and I would need to keep her safe with me until I found out what was going on in the lunchroom.

I couldn't quite believe what had just taken place. If other staff members had walked by my classroom at that moment and seen a student kicking my chair, and then heard me respond positively with an invitation to lunch, they might have found it rather unusual. Why would I reward "bad behaviour?" they might have asked. In fact, when I described this experience to other staff members later that day, several of them responded in disbelief, and warned me that I had made a big mistake. Common practice dictated that "bad behaviour," like kicking a chair, must be discouraged, and rewarding it would make it more difficult to stop the behaviour in the future. How lucky that no one had walked by my class at that moment!

I often hear that I must have had a great deal of patience when working with my students; I always respond by saying it was actually the students who needed to be patient with me as I muddled my way through and tried to figure things out. When a student is afraid and can't explain what is wrong, and then becomes frustrated and frightened, it is understanding and discretion that are often required.

Later that day, I made inquiries among the lunchroom staff and was told that a new student in the lunchroom had been bothering Angel. But given her quiet nature, the staff had failed to realize how upset she was, and no one had intervened. Angel had responded appropriately, ignoring the student and not reacting to taunts during these unpleasant lunchroom experiences, but her self-control was mistaken for not being bothered by the new student. If she had reacted and yelled during these lunchroom interactions, perhaps her needs would have been recognized and efforts to resolve the situation would have followed.

To assume that Angel was not upset by the taunts of another student because she did not react was to assume she had no feelings; this points to how much our students are misunderstood. Bullying is never acceptable under any circumstances, and doing nothing creates a culture where bullying is allowed to take hold.

Angel's dreaded anticipation of returning to the lunchroom, which resulted in her kicking my chair, was deserving of understanding rather than punishment. I hadn't been listening carefully to Angel when she first indicated that she was upset, and instead assumed that she merely wanted reassurance about the schedule. Thankfully, Angel felt safe expressing her fear to me outside of the lunchroom, and I'm glad I was finally able to "hear" her message and offer support.

Angel and I enjoyed a pleasant lunch together that afternoon, and I told the other students in the class they too could join us for lunch in our classroom if they needed a break from their regular routine; the choice was theirs. Many of my students took me up on the offer, and they realized that having the ability to change their own schedule or routine and having the opportunity to make choices actually gave them more control than a rigid schedule did. Giving students opportunities to make choices in their daily lives will help them develop a sense of independence and autonomy, along with an even greater sense of security. And our students will soon begin to realize that they can rely on themselves.

Schedules are great, but an overreliance on them can create the very problems and behaviours we wish to discourage in the first place, resulting in frustration and meltdowns when things inevitably change. It is important to introduce and teach students from an early age how schedules can be flexible, thereby teaching them to be flexible themselves. Giving students choices and asking for their input on other matters may better prepare them for life and the inevitable detours they will encounter along the way. It is important that we remain vigilant and do not inadvertently overuse strategies or techniques that work in the short term but may become problematic later on.

If I hadn't figured out what was bothering Angel, I might have said she was simply having a bad day, or that she kicked the chair "for no apparent reason." But I've never been comfortable with statements like that—they are unhelpful and often prevent us from gaining a deeper understanding about what is really going on, as if "for no apparent reason" is an answer in itself. Even after I explained the circumstances surrounding Angel's outburst, many professionals I spoke to still believed that this behaviour would likely be repeated, and a consequence was what was required. But that truly would have been a lost opportunity for real understanding and connection. The outburst was uncharacteristic of Angel, and in the years she remained in my class it never was repeated. By responding to the source of Angel's fear and anxiety, rather than simply responding to the apparently inappropriate behaviour of kicking the chair, of the "acting self," I was able to understand my student, and together we could solve the problem. This helped establish a relationship of trust, where even when words fail, understanding remains. And isn't it this deep and meaningful human connection that we are trying to establish? After that day, we continued to enjoy many lunches together and the food never tasted so sweet.

There were many occasions when I was not able to figure out what was bothering my students, but I kept trying. There was always a reason, even if it wasn't apparent at first. Therein lies the challenge to continue to "do better."

4

Good Days and Bad
Reducing Anxiety
and Enhancing Learning

OVER THE YEARS, I have noticed that while many of my students presented with a wide range of needs and behaviours, they all had one trait in common: they all experienced extreme levels of anxiety and fear. The greater the anxiety, the more pronounced their symptoms or behaviours became. The symptoms or behaviours therefore seemed to ebb and flow along with their level of anxiety and their ability to cope with the world around them. Symptoms or behaviours are often a consequence of the coping mechanisms individuals develop to help them deal with their core issues. Too often people try to treat the symptoms, rather than the reasons for them, and end up creating more problems than they solve.

Before we even begin to plan our important work, it is critical that we focus on the "why"—the reason for certain behaviours—rather than simply following a checklist and then deciding "what" behaviour we will focus on next. Teachers and other professionals need to understand the nature of these behaviours before deciding whether they should be eliminated altogether. They should also consider whether the behaviour should be modified, redirected, or supported by other helpful strategies (such as sensory therapy) or by modifying the environment (like with Irlen lenses/filters, appropriate computer screens, caps with brims to lessen impact of bright lights).

The term *autism* is derived from the classical Greek *auto* for "self"—so, "selfism." I believe this term, as it has come to be understood, can be somewhat misleading, for it suggests a "fixed" and "inner" state of being, a condition to be cured. A more accurate and dynamic understanding of autism recognizes its interconnectedness with the outer world, a heightened sense of self rather than a disconnection from self. It recognizes the presentation of autistic traits as the *consequence* of autism, thereby capturing the dynamic nature of ASD and the ebb and flow of responses.

What we often observe is a child's retreat into self as a consequence of being *too* connected to the world around them. It is the child's experience *of* and *in* a heightened and overwhelming awareness of the world around them, rather than a lack of awareness of it, that can result in the retreat into themselves. Autism is the place where they end up, not where they begin or must remain. In fact, I would go as far as to argue that autism is actually the opposite of what the term suggests, that it is a consequence of being overly connected with the world, and becoming overwhelmed by the sensory experience of it, which then results in disconnection.

Temple Grandin expresses this beautifully in her book *Emergence: Labeled Autistic* (2005) when she writes about her own experience. "Emergence" in the title reflects a dynamic and promising pathway toward discovering and enhancing the potential within. I very much like Grandin's definition of autism in this book as well, because it shows us how to design more meaningful and effective interventions and strategies as our students begin to learn and discover their true potential, and begin to *emerge* beyond their "inner world" and "reach out and explore the world":

> Autism is a developmental disorder. A defect in the systems which process incoming sensory information causes the child to over-react to some stimuli and under-react to others. The autistic child often withdraws from her environment and the people in it to block out an onslaught of incoming stimulation. Autism is a childhood anomaly that separates the child from interpersonal relationships. She does not reach out and explore the world around her, but instead stays in her own inner world.

The ebb and flow of the expression of autistic traits/behaviours is a good sign. Good days and bad days point to the dynamic nature of autism as a response to the world and to its effect on the lives of individuals who must continually adapt to and cope with constant impacts on the senses. Understanding sensory issues is an important step toward addressing these challenges.

BERNARD RIMLAND

IN 1964, American psychologist Bernard Rimland published his groundbreaking book, *Infantile Autism: The Syndrome and Its Implications for a Neural Theory of Behavior*. The book represented a radical departure from the common practice of blaming parents, offering instead a science-based biological theory that explored the core characteristics of autism in relation to the brain. This major shift in perspective would not only impact how autism was understood, but also offer important insights for the development of new treatments and remedial interventions. Now the focus would be on understanding the child, and this new understanding would improve the lives of countless families and their children. Rimland also recognized the valuable and important role parents could play in their child's care and development, encouraging them to become part of the solution, since they were no longer viewed as part of the problem. Those days were finally coming to an end, and there was new hope on the horizon.

In recognition of the importance of Rimland's book, a fiftieth-anniversary edition was published in 2015, including new contributions from leading experts in the field of autism today. In the foreword to the anniversary edition, Temple Grandin describes the impact the book had on her life when it was first published. In her twenties at the time, Grandin discovered in Rimland's book a new theory of autism that finally made sense to her personally: "When his book was first published, he was a lone visionary... In the 1960s, most doctors still believed that there was a psychological basis to my symptoms... Throughout elementary school, my psychiatrist kept attempting to find my 'psychic injury'... changing his opinion when he observed that my sister, who was only a year and a half younger, was developing normally. From this he concluded that my 'autistic symptoms' were not caused by 'bad mothering'" (Rimland [1964] 2015, 15). At last, Rimland provided Grandin with some answers, along with explanations for her sensory sensitivities and her need for deep pressure. "I was relieved to find out from this book that autism was a biological disorder and not a psychological problem," she wrote.

Rimland's insights about autism and parenting were also very personal. In 1956, shortly after the birth of their son, Mark, Rimland and his wife, Gloria, began to notice that Mark wasn't responding or behaving like other infants. They became very worried and consulted various pediatricians but still couldn't figure out what was wrong. Then one day Gloria remembered reading a psychology textbook that described children who acted differently; she found the book and the appropriate section, and they realized their son had autism. Even with his background—having recently completed a doctoral degree in experimental psychology—Rimland was not familiar with the term.

Rimland then took it upon himself to find everything he could about autism and to figure out how to help his son. At the time, he was working full-time as a researcher for the US Navy and could spend only evenings and weekends on his research. He set up a makeshift home office in what had been the side porch of their small house. Soon books and articles piled up as Rimland set about solving the mystery of autism. During the course of his own research, he soon became aware of the prevalence of poorly conceived research promoting the "refrigerator mother" theory that had been accepted by many health-care professionals around the world. Refusing to accept blame for his son's condition, Rimland became even more determined to figure out how to help him. His hard work, love and dedication paid off, and eight years after Mark's birth, Bernard Rimland's seminal book was published. Now countless families and professionals could finally begin to make a real difference in the lives of so many deserving children.

Rimland's book would greatly influence the field of autism research and lead to the development of new approaches and resources. He developed one of the first checklists to help families and professionals identify autistic characteristics, and also paved the way to the development of Applied Behaviour Analysis (ABA), now widely recognized as an effective approach in helping children during the early and critical years of development.

In 1965, Rimland and Ruth Sullivan, a parent activist with an autistic child, established the National Society for Autistic Children (NSAC) to advocate on behalf of special needs children. Sullivan became its first president and began organizing concerned parents to advocate for universal access to public education for all special needs children. Early on, Rimland and the NSAC recognized the important role education could play in the lives of children with different learning needs and styles of learning. Yet in 2020, parents around the world still find that they must continue to advocate for the educational needs and rights of their children.

Bernard Rimland died in November 2006, aged 78. His legacy lives on in the ongoing neuroscientific research that continues to explore the inner workings of "the autistic brain." But what mattered most was his commitment to improving the lives of family members in their struggle to meet the needs of children who are often still so misunderstood.

Today, Mark Rimland is in his sixties and lives in the neighbourhood where he grew up in San Diego. He is well known in the community, and can often be seen strolling the streets, visiting friends and drinking herbal tea at his favorite hangouts. He is also a well-established artist, having discovered his artistic abilities in his early twenties, when he attended his first art class—a perfect example of the importance of lifelong learning and the discovery of hidden potential. Mark spends much of his time at a nearby training centre for adults with developmental disabilities, which also runs an off-site art gallery, where Mark is a resident artist. He enjoys life and is an active member of his community.

Mark also has what is known as a calendar memory, the ability to determine the day of the week of any calendar date—allowing him to name the day a person was born once he is given their birthdate. This is often referred to as a savant skill, and it became an important part of Bernard Rimland's research. In chapter 10 of his book, he refers to "the special abilities of autism," identifying children with special skills in areas such as music, art, puzzle tasks, spatial abilities, calendar calculating, or exceptional memory skills. Individuals with such abilities were often referred to as "idiot savants," an unfortunate and outdated term that was eventually changed to "savant syndrome" at the suggestion of Darold Treffert, a psychiatrist and leading expert in this field. Treffert's commentary on Rimland's work appears in the fiftieth-anniversary edition of *Infantile Autism* and provides a crucial update to this important area of research.

CAREY 2006   Rimland (1964) 2015; Shattock 2006

Oops

The *ish* lesson got me thinking about other ways I might lessen the anxiety level of my students during problematic situations. When things went wrong, even my highly verbal students seemed unable to express their needs or process what I was saying as I tried to reason with them. My words no longer conveyed meaning in their increased state of anxiety and fear, because in these situations they experienced a heightened sense of the world as being either black or white, good or bad, safe or dangerous. Typical people who fear elevators or planes may experience a similar level of anxiety when there is no clear or present danger—try reasoning with a friend or family member who suffers from claustrophobia and is stuck on an elevator and you will realize that your words go unheard.

Perhaps if the students and I came up with a sound or words that would quickly convey that everything was okay, I thought, I might be able to penetrate their anxious state and help them navigate life's grey areas.

And that's when I introduced *oops*. At first, we practiced by acting out simple mistakes. I dropped a book and then laughed as I said "*oops*." Without being prompted, the entire class laughed and said *oops* as I continued dropping the book. Then I encouraged the students to copy my actions and we all dropped our books as we giggled *oops*. We continued with other minor mistakes and mishaps followed by *oops*, reinforcing that these mishaps were not very serious. We began to spontaneously use *oops* as events naturally occurred during our daily routines. When we got really good, we could even combine *oops* with *ish*—as in, "*Oops*, the bus will be late today and won't arrive until 4-*ish*." As silly as you might think this strategy sounds, it really worked—and it was fun. How nice to finally hear laughter instead of tears when the bus arrived late. *Ish* and *oops* quickly conveyed that the situation was not serious, and the anxiety disappeared.

Ben: Out of Batteries

One of my students was terrified during an ice storm and resulting three-day power outage, when the city was thrown into total darkness. He began to associate any breakdown of computers, machines, and other equipment with catastrophe.

One day, as Ben was using a stationary bike in the gym, the bike suddenly stopped working. Fear and panic took hold, and *oops* did not reassure him. I quickly improvised and added, "Out of batteries!" and it worked. I don't even know if the bike actually used batteries, but the message conveyed that the breakdown wasn't serious. Ben calmly got off the bike and found another one that worked just fine. No long-winded explanations, just a simple message to help interpret the complex unpredictable and confusing world around us.

"Out of batteries" became a useful strategy. We added a visual sign, "*Oops*—Out of Order," which was always nearby, just in case.

I had a few other "short and sweet" techniques that helped reduce my students' anxiety. For example, one strategy that worked well with some students was to sing their name when they appeared anxious. It seemed to awaken their calmer self and connect with another part of the brain, and I would continue to sing my instructions until they relaxed. Another technique that I found useful was to play the same soft music I used during our relaxation exercises when difficult situations and upsets took place in class. This seemed to remind them to relax and use their calming breathing skills. The sound of familiar and relaxing music quickly conveyed far more than mere words could.

"Don't Forget Your Change"

When students are anxious, it is difficult for them to focus on school activities and participate in learning. Often, when the social dimension is added to a learning task, it can raise the level of anxiety even more and interfere with learning the new skill. Again, it is not unlike trying to teach a person with a fear of elevators the Pythagorean theorem while riding in an elevator; it just won't work. I have often found it helpful to separate the social from the cognitive task and combine them only once the new skill has been mastered. This can be useful when preparing students for co-op placements that may require them to interact with the public.

There was a vending machine in the school cafeteria that provided water, soft drinks, and juice. Many of my students had money and often would purchase a drink from the machine rather than buying one from a person in the school cafeteria, as they found it less stressful. However, when I watched them using the machine, I noticed that they often guessed at the amount of coins that were needed for the purchase, and if they "got lucky" and a drink was dispensed, they simply took their drink and walked away, not realizing they were owed change. I realized this would be the perfect opportunity to teach them how to conduct money exchanges. Their luck was about to change.

Leaving the human factor out of the equation at first, I would use the vending machine, which they already liked, as a method for teaching math and financial transactions. I ran to the caretaker's storage locker and found two giant cardboard boxes that would be perfect for designing and building our own classroom vending machine to dispense healthy drinks and snacks. With the help of a handy educational assistant and interested students, we created our very own "human" vending machine, complete with money slot, change chamber, and dispensing chute, as well as an opening at the back where a more capable student would stand hidden from view to help complete the transaction. The students enjoyed participating in the creation of our classroom vending machine, and this awakened their interest in planning and designing other projects.

The front of the vending machine was designed to be part of a dynamic math lesson for figuring out the amount required to pay for the items listed on the front of the machine. To assist the students in figuring out the proper change, Velcro-backed cards (easily swapped out to match a given student's level of ability) were placed beside a picture of the item to be purchased, right on the front of the machine. Beside the photo were pictures of coins and calculations, to help the students with their transactions. The cards and calculations were designed incrementally, introducing more difficult transactions as their skills improved. Eventually no tutorial cards would be required. Supplementary pencil and paper exercises, along with games such as Money Bingo, helped the students develop their math skills.

Since the students had varying levels of ability, the more advanced students stood inside the "machine" to check the accuracy of the change. At first, students were expected to use the exact change in order to purchase their item, and only later were they to use coins that would require them to calculate the change they should expect. Sometimes, as is typical in real vending machines, no change appeared (a strategy used to test the students), and they had to say "out of order" or point to the "out of order" sign to indicate that they were waiting for their change. As their skills improved, students took turns standing inside the machine. It seemed that both receiving and dispensing an item was equally rewarding. When the correct transaction resulted in a drink or a healthy snack, everyone felt like a winner as they cheered together and gave the reminder, "Don't forget your change!"

"Money Makes the World Go Round"

I always taught money math using real money, as the physical nature of coins in particular reinforced both tactile and visual memory skills, along with the cognitive aspect of the task. Sometimes I asked the students to place different coins in their pockets as part of a game and then asked them to pull out the different coins I asked for without looking. They could also jingle their change if they felt anxious, as this is an acceptable (if annoying) habit of many people.

We also played Money Bingo to practice and reinforce calculations, and this helped instill an association between fun and enjoyment and the daily math transactions. The students loved doing these activities and gradually became more comfortable and familiar with handling money, which would help reduce their anxiety during real-life transactions.

The students could now use the cafeteria vending machine with ease, but only as a last resort; they seemed to prefer our personal classroom version, which never kept your money or needed a shake.

Even when they mastered money exchanges using the vending machine, several still experienced anxiety when making purchases in stores. So we rehearsed making purchases in class with each other in order to move from the familiar to the less familiar. I am a big fan of student-run stores and feel they provide much-needed practice and experience in preparation for both co-op placements and shopping in the community. The earlier students start, the better. One class of entrepreneurial students sold coffee, tea, hot chocolate, and homemade baked goods every lunch hour, and the funds helped pay for a class trip to the local Mennonite farmers' market.

Students selling to students seems to lessen anxiety levels and helps to develop close social connections and friendships. Making purchases at a farmers' market now seemed far less daunting for the students, something to look forward to rather than be feared.

DEAL ME IN!

ONE OF my favourite classroom resources was an old favourite from the 1970s called *Deal Me In! The Use of Playing Cards in Teaching and Learning*, by Margie Golick, a talented and insightful psychologist and former senior psychologist at Montreal Children's Hospital's Learning Centre.

Golick would often engage in a game of cards with children as an important part of her psychoeducational assessment. Not only did the game put the children at ease, but more importantly, it also provided Golick with an opportunity to observe them in a more natural and relaxed setting. It is amazing how much a psychometrist or teacher can learn from observing students playing cards. This was an important part of my training in informal assessment and programming for determining individual student strengths and needs.

In her book, Golick skillfully demonstrates how a simple deck of cards can become an invaluable teaching tool for developing learning skills, fine and gross motor skills, eye-hand co-ordination, organizational habits, social skills, and—most important of all— having fun. I always had several decks of cards on hand in the classroom; we especially loved our giant-sized deck. Golick's book includes over eighty card games, complete with rules. Of course, my students loved the rules, which provided a wonderful anchor as they learned to interact with others and take turns. The "rules of engagement" that card games provide help establish a wonderful framework through which many friendships developed. When students find it difficult to interact spontaneously, a good card game can set things in motion. Fish, anyone?

5

The Tide Is Turning

LIFE IS FULL of surprises. When I first started teaching students with developmental needs, including many with autism spectrum characteristics, I discovered that my students and I were in fact more alike than different. This was contrary to what I had been taught as part of my teacher training, where "different" and "special" were emphasized, while sameness or commonality were not even considered relevant. However, as I came to know and understand my students, I realized that their behavioural characteristics represented many aspects of most people's personalities writ large—characteristics and traits that we (neurotypicals) had learned to control and keep in check, lest we offend. Yes, people with ASD may have difficulty controlling certain behaviours, but we all possess these characteristics and desires in varying degrees.

In a *National Post* article in 2006, Wendy Roberts, a world-renowned developmental pediatrician and international leader in autism research, said, "I think of autism as being a difference in wiring. It is like a collection of otherwise normal 'quirks' that are taken to such an extreme that they impair a person's ability to function. But it is still 'on a continuum of normal.'" Professor emerita at the University of Toronto and currently the clinical director at Integrated Services for Autism and Neurodevelopmental Disorders (ISAND), Roberts is an advocate for providing meaningful services within a collaborative framework of integrated disciplines.

In an interview with the *Huffington Post* about what motivated her to write *The Autistic Brain*, Temple Grandin (2014) expressed similar thinking: "I had done all these brain scans. Also I wanted to go into a lot more detail on the different kinds of brains. The visual thinkers, the math thinkers and the word thinkers. And talk about the research that shows that's really true, that there really are different kinds of minds and they can work together."

ISAND is a wonderful program, offering "developmental medical care, language and social communication therapies, occupational and behavioural therapies, diet and nutrition as well as mental health and wellness supports for individuals and families" in Toronto.

isand.ca

Perhaps we are beginning to understand that we are more alike than different: we all fall somewhere along the continuum. This is a good thing, for we need different minds in our ever-changing world. We need each other. Understanding this made me question the conventional wisdom about autism and the role I should play as a teacher in this field. While I don't wish to downplay the serious challenges we face when addressing the needs of students with extreme expressions of ASD, I found myself asking what the students' true needs were versus our needs, and how we could reconcile the two without sacrificing the giftedness or extraordinary aspects of our students in the process. In the current school culture, there is an expectation that those who are "different" should be made more like us (or more "normal'), so that they fit in. But couldn't we make some changes ourselves and meet somewhere in the middle, so that special traits and abilities aren't lost in the process? Couldn't we begin to see "different" as "exceptional," as we now often refer to special needs, by finally recognizing and accepting the exceptional and *extraordinary* as an important opportunity to be explored and developed? I don't believe it has to be all or nothing—not either/or, but both/and.

Larry: A Cautionary Tale

Temple Grandin reminds us to "see the person, not the label":

This issue is explored in depth in Steve Silberman's wonderful 2015 book, *Neuro-Tribes: The Legacy of Autism and the Future of Neurodiversity.*

Do not get hung up on labels. Labels are useful for obtaining services ... but the label should never define the child nor dictate what program should be used with the child. Autism spectrum disorders are varied and no two individuals will manifest the same set of characteristics at the same level of intensity. Always look at the child—not the label—and base treatment decisions on the child's individual profile of strengths and weaknesses, learning style, personality, etc ... NEVER let a label lower your reasonable expectations of a child and that child's capacity for learning. By doing so, you rob the child of the very experiences and opportunities that can allow learning to grow and develop. You rob the child of his potential, and his future. All because of a label? ... Let us not limit the lives of these children and adults by our own preconceived notions based on the label attached to them. See the person, not the label. (2008, 9–10)

While I certainly recognize the importance of labels and diagnoses in securing funding, I also believe we must always keep their limitations in mind to prevent them from interfering with learning and development. The story of Larry has stayed with me over the years as a reminder of how problematic labels can be.

Larry was a quiet, strapping fifteen-year-old who kept to himself. He had been enrolled for a few years in a high school non-credit life-skills program for students with developmental delays when his teachers began to notice a change in his quiet nature. He became more and more restless and anxious in class, and began to display angry outbursts "for no apparent reason." He started skipping school and had a few run-ins with the law for vandalism, luckily getting off with a warning. Without looking into what might be behind this change in Larry's behaviour, the staff felt that a change in teachers rather than a change in program might help. He was transferred to my life-skills class for students with developmental differences.

It was a beautiful fall day in October when Larry joined our class, looking very unhappy. We were heading to our classroom garden to plant daffodil, tulip, and allium bulbs. The previous year, we had reclaimed a neglected patch of earth in the rear parking lot and turned it into an oasis of colourful flowers, along with delicious vegetables like squash, tomatoes, and even one little pumpkin. Herbs like oregano and dill also thrived. (We knew our garden was a real success when rabbits began to appear, nibbling on the "fruits of our labour.")

I began to review the life cycle of plants with the students, but before I could finish explaining how the energy of the sun awakens the green colour hidden in the leaves of the plant, Larry interrupted and said, "Oh, you mean photosynthesis."

"Yes," I quickly answered. "Where did you learn about it?"

"In a magazine," he replied.

When I questioned Larry further, he explained that several years ago he had found a pile of old *National Geographic* and science magazines beside the dumpster at his apartment building. He kept them and read them over and over again, also enjoying the photographs.

Until Larry joined my class, his education had primarily focused on doing simple life-skills exercises and tasks, and he had not been exposed to more challenging academic work. I asked him where he had learned to read so well and he said, "I don't know, I just read." Could he have taught himself to read at an early age, I wondered? (See chapter 7 for more on hyperlexia.)

I usually wait until I get to know a student before reviewing their complete school records and history, in order to keep an open mind. But I felt it was important to break with this practice and figure out why Larry was even in a non-credit life-skills program. I requested more information from the school records and eventually received a copy of his original assessment, conducted five years earlier, along with a more recent assessment. Both reports used the Pervasive Development Disorder–Not Otherwise Specified (PDD-NOS) designation to describe Larry's difficulties. (I always found this label confusing, and thankfully it was not included in the DSM-5.[1])

Larry's situation points to the confusion that can result when educators rely too much on labels and recommendations from mental health professionals, which they may accept at face value. In addition, many mental health professionals are unfamiliar with the variety of programs offered and associated terminology used at the high school level, and may wrongly assume that a high school placement means that students are earning credits toward a high school diploma.

Treatment centres, with the best of intentions, may recommend small, self-contained classroom settings without realizing that many of these programs are in fact non-credit.

Many parents I've encountered over the years have told me they too were surprised to discover that their child who had behavioural or social concerns, but who had strengths and abilities in other areas, was not earning any high school credits. Larry's mother, a single parent who had never completed high school herself, also believed her son was earning credits and was shocked to discover he was not working toward earning his high school diploma. "His report card said he was doing so well and passing," she said. "I don't understand." In fact, both Larry's recent and earlier psychoeducational assessments indicated that he fell within the range of normal intellectual functioning, and both reports identified his potential for academic success in high school. So how did he end up in a non-credit life-skills program?

The original assessment was made when Larry was ten years old. At the time, his mother had become concerned for her son's safety, as he seemed to have no sense of danger and displayed poor judgment when crossing the street and riding his bike. He loved climbing onto roofs in his neighbourhood. The report labelled Larry with PDD-NOS and recommended that he be placed in a small, well-supervised behavioural classroom within a treatment facility focused on addressing concerning behaviour. His strengths and educational needs were set aside in order to address what were viewed as more pressing issues.

In a treatment program, Larry's behavioural problems improved and he learned to be more cautious and to control his reckless behaviour. However, the "behaviour" label remained, resulting in his transfer from the treatment facility to another behavioural program for Grades 7 and 8, and from there into a small non-credit high school life-skills program for students with behavioural and developmental needs.

Once labels and program designations take hold, it can be hard to break free from their tenacious grip.

Looking at Larry's file, I believed that the words *developmental disorder* embedded in the PDD-NOS label may have somehow overshadowed his academic strengths and potential, making the deficits and worrisome behaviours the determining factor in his program placements.

Since both the current and past assessments had identified Larry's strengths and abilities, and the potential for academic success, the school psychologist I spoke with recommended a change in program and a plan to carefully begin a gradual transition to credit classes. Now that I had the go-ahead, I gladly modified Larry's program, introducing more challenging, credit-based work to prepare him for the transition to credit classes. The transition was a great success. I stayed in touch with Larry's new teachers, and they reported that he was happy and making excellent progress. Larry was thrilled with his more challenging program and, according to his mother, was happier than he'd been in years. The worrying behaviours that had landed him in my class were now a thing of the past. He was learning, pursuing his passions—he was happy.

After a year in a credit program, Larry transitioned to a computer programming class at a technical high school alongside a co-op placement in a photography lab, his interest in photography having been awakened years before by those discarded *National Geographic* magazines. A few years after Larry graduated, I ran into him on the subway and he told me he was working as a computer assistant in a photography studio and loved his new job. I wished him much success as we waved goodbye.

Unfortunately, Larry's experience is not unique. I witnessed similar misunderstandings around student placements over the years. Once a label is applied, with a focus on deficits and behaviours and with less attention paid to strengths and abilities, a student may be denied an opportunity to find and reach their potential. Luckily, Larry did achieve academic success, but it was more by chance than design, and that simply is not good enough. Despite our best intentions, deficit-based models can actually interfere with learning potential. Strength-based programs are more open-ended and offer more opportunities to grow and learn. It is not always easy to determine a student's potential, particularly when challenging behaviours interfere with the learning process. But acknowledging strengths and respecting interests has always brought out the best in my students, and helped them develop a love of learning.

The misunderstandings associated with Larry's experience and school placement should remind us to look past the label and to consider needs and *abilities*. Seeing the person and not the label is the key. I always look to the strengths to guide me and have never been led astray.

Ravi: A World of Possibilities

A change in mindset opens up a world of possibilities. I was reminded of that lesson by another student, named Ravi, whose teachers believed in him and not the label. Ravi decided to share his personal experience and wrote a moving article, "The Path of a True Lion," for our school newspaper, *The Lion's Pulse* (Spring 2014). I'd like to close Part I of this book with an excerpt:

> I started here five years ago in the Developmentally Delayed (DD) Program but switched over to mainstream classes about two years ago... I want to take a moment

to tell you what it is like to be a Special Needs student...
where students are pushed to perform to the best of their
abilities. The teachers in this department understand that
these students are capable of far more than they give themselves credit for. DD students work hard; they learn and
make great progress on a daily basis. Unfortunately, it is
often difficult for people outside the program to see their
achievements... I believe that students in the mainstream
don't always take the time to look at what Special Needs
students can do; instead only seeing what we cannot do.
I think that sometimes, students still think that those who
rely on the DD/PD [Developmentally Delayed/Physically
Disabled] department possess little in the way of "abilities," and that we—and thus everything we do—are vastly
different from what the rest of Monarch Park's student
body does...

Monarch Park's Special Needs students are all unique
and amazing individuals who deserve the same, if not more,
recognition for all they do on a daily basis. We are capable
of more than we are credited with and if you take a moment
to notice, you will see us and all we do.

RAVI MAHARAJ

Rethinking Behaviour

SPECTRUM: SPECial TRaits of unique Minds

Our current view of autism as part of a broad and multidimensional spectrum of traits can be traced back to 1979, when British child psychiatrist Lorna Wing and her colleague, psychologist Judith Gould, first introduced this new and revolutionary understanding of autism. Over the course of their research, they came to realize that it was the children who *didn't* fit into neat little categories who offered the greatest insights and would help them develop the concept, which was more like a spectrum. As a result, they placed less emphasis on "giving a name to the condition" than on "identifying all the needs a person has" and, by association, the supports that would help them reach their potential (Ayris 2013, 33).

Almost forty years after its introduction, the concept of an expanded autism spectrum was finally added to the Diagnostic and Statistical Manual (DSM-5) in 2013—a tribute to Wing and Gould's foresight and wisdom as we continue to move closer to understanding the complexities and the hidden potential of the human mind and brain.

Wing and Gould first described their view of autism as a broad and diverse *continuum*. They later revised it, describing it as a *spectrum* disorder, reflecting a more nuanced and dimensional understanding. As Gould (Feinstein 2010, 153) explained, "We first called it the 'autistic continuum' and then we realized that the word *continuum* had an implication of discrete descriptions along a line, whereas that was not what it really was. It was not a question of moving in severity from very severe to mild. That was not what we were trying to get across. The concept of a spectrum is more like a spectrum of light, with blurring."

The second half of this book is dedicated to developing an expanded understanding of the autism spectrum in all its forms and aspects. Today, the concept of an autism spectrum may help redirect our focus from the label to the individual and their needs. As we continue to broaden our understanding of "thinking across the spectrum" and beyond, we can begin to achieve "what could be better."

"THE KEY to autism is the key to the nature of human life... The reward for the effort involved is a deeper understanding of human social interaction and an appreciation of the wonder of child development."

LORNA WING

6

See the Child,
Not the Label

LORNA WING and Judith Gould developed their understanding of the diverse needs and abilities of individuals with autism over the course of their Camberwell Register study (1972–79), based on data collected from the Camberwell area of South London (Wing and Gould 1979). They reviewed patient records, looking for children under the age of fifteen with "any kind of physical or psychological disability or abnormality of behaviour, however mild or severe" (L. Wing 2001, xiii). They subsequently interviewed the families and their children and, contrary to what they expected, soon realized that the current diagnostic labels were too restrictive and did not reflect the varied and diverse aspects of the children's conditions. For it was their differences as well as their similarities that made the greatest impression on Wing and Gould.

Lorna Wing's interest in autism was very personal. In 1959, her daughter, Susie, then three years old, was diagnosed with autism. It was only by chance that Wing became aware of the work of Leo Kanner, who in 1943 introduced the diagnostic term *early infantile autism* to describe eleven children who came to his clinic. Kanner (1943) profiled the children in his landmark paper, "Autistic Disturbances of Affective Contact." Wing's psychiatric training had barely touched on autism, but once she discovered Kanner's research she realized that "it was obvious that Susie had classic Kanner's autism." Wing (2001, xi–xii) summarized the central features of Kanner's diagnosis as a "profound lack of affective (emotional) contact with other people; intense insistence on sameness in their self-chosen, often bizarre and elaborate repetitive routines; mutism or marked abnormality of speech; fascination with and dexterity in manipulating objects; high levels of visual-spatial skills or rote memory in contrast to learning difficulties in other areas; an attractive, alert, intelligent appearance." She also noted, "It seems likely that there have always been autistic children... Perhaps they were the reason for the legends of 'fairy changeling' children" (1972, 6). At the time, these children were given little notice and were simply dismissed as odd, feeble-minded or eccentric. They would only come to our attention a decade after child psychiatry was first established as a specialty, in 1930, at the Johns Hopkins pediatric hospital in Baltimore. Kanner was appointed as the department's head, thereby making him the first child psychiatrist in the United States. As concerned parents learned of this new clinic, they began to bring their children to Kanner and his team with the hope that this new discipline might have the answers they were seeking. Thirteen years later, Kanner would introduce the new diagnosis of *infantile autism* and the emerging discipline of child psychiatry. Like Wing, he acknowledged that he "did not discover autism. It was there before" (Donvan and Zucker 2016, 38).

Soon after Susie's diagnosis, Lorna Wing devoted her professional efforts to autism research and switched her specialty to child psychiatry. She advanced a more scientifically based understanding of autism, as a new awareness was emerging: "1960 saw the start of a marked change in ideas about autism. The work of researchers in Britain and the U.S. was beginning to show that the behaviour of children with autism made most sense if viewed as the result of developmental disorders, starting from birth or the early years of childhood. Growing knowledge of brain function pointed to biological causes" (2001, xii).

In 1966, Lorna's husband, John Wing, who was also a psychiatrist, edited the book *Early Childhood Autism: Clinical, Educational and Social Aspects*, further expanding the current understanding of autism. In the title, he replaced Kanner's term *infantile* with *early childhood*, thereby capturing the more developmental nature of the condition. The rest of the title highlighted the importance of including professionals from various disciplines, as well as parents and educators, so as to gain a broader understanding of the condition. John Wing also recognized the advantage of using a multidisciplinary approach, which would better address the daily lives of children. The book included an eclectic selection of articles from different disciplines, each using distinctive approaches but all sharing a common point of view—that if help is offered early, "the child's disabilities [can be] minimized by skilled remedial teaching" rather than by seeing the child as "hopeless" and placing them in an "unsuitable institution" (J. Wing [1966] 1969, xi).

"Nature Never Draws a Line without Smudging It"

Lorna Wing's personal connection with autism helped her more easily recognize children like her daughter, Susie, who fit Kanner's diagnosis. However, Wing (2001, xiii) and Gould noticed something else: while they "could identify a group with typical Kanner's autism... [they] also found many others who had features of autistic behaviour but who did not precisely fit Kanner's criteria." Again, it was the children who didn't fit into neat little categories who offered the greatest insights and who would help them develop the concept of the autism spectrum.

As Wing and Gould continued their work in Camberwell, they saw that strictly defined labels and designated categories did not represent or serve the needs of the individuals they were meeting, nor did they reflect their unique and personal expression of autism. Instead, they saw the value of recognizing individual differences, which had been ignored by the limitations of narrow and oversimplified labels. A broadened view would expand our understanding and appreciation for the person, their needs, and their strengths, thereby allowing for meaningful remedial interventions. The label would need to change to accommodate and serve the needs of the individual, rather than forcing the individual into fixed categories that limit opportunities for dynamic growth, development, and true understanding.

As Wing and Gould continued to meet with the families in their Camberwell study, they began to notice other individuals who did not seem to fit into any category, although they too had social deficits and displayed many autistic characteristics. But as luck would have it, halfway through their research, they found the answer they were looking for.

John Wing became aware of a paper written in 1944, in German, by a relatively unknown Austrian pediatrician, Hans Asperger. Since no English translation existed, John, who just happened to be fluent in German, excitedly translated it for his wife. In his paper, "Die autistischen Psychopathen im Kindesalter" ("Autistic Psychopathy in Childhood"),[1] Asperger described a group of children and adolescents with the following characteristics: "naïve, inappropriate social approaches to others; intense circumscribed interest in particular subjects such as railway timetables; good grammar and vocabulary but monotonous speech used for monologues, not two-way conversations; poor motor coordination; level of ability in the borderline, average or superior range but often with specific learning difficulties in one or two subjects; a marked lack of common sense" (L. Wing 2001, xiii). Asperger's research would add yet another significant dimension of complexity to the ever-evolving concept of the spectrum. The lines of the continuum were continuing to blur.[2]

Lorna Wing was always cautious about diagnostic labels, seeing them as useful only for getting people the services they needed. She was often quoted as saying, "You cannot separate into those 'with' and 'without' traits as they are so scattered..." (Rhodes 2011) and "We need to see each child as an individual" (*Telegraph* 2014).

The chapters to come, on hyperlexia (self-taught early reading), echolalia (repeating words, phrases, and expressions), eye contact, and perception, will take a closer look at these traits in more neurological and developmental terms to help dispel many of the misconceptions surrounding them. Once viewed from the perspective of the "thinking self," these traits will no longer appear simply as odd and meaningless behaviours; rather, they will be seen as opportunities for further growth and development within an appropriate educational framework. As I describe how my students process information and the way their perceptual tendencies help shape their responses to the environment, we will begin to move a little closer to understanding the challenges they encounter in their daily lives. Their "behaviours" can then be considered from a very different perspective, offering insights that have often been overlooked or dismissed as inconsequential.

By listening to my students and their parents, I realized that I still had a lot to learn about the diverse special traits of unique minds and the many different ways we all perceive and experience the world. As I present their experiences in these chapters, a new awareness of sensory perception and different ways of experiencing the world will emerge. My students will teach us how to see things differently as we navigate their world together. Once we begin to see things from the inside out rather than just from the outside, from the perspective of the "thinking self" rather than the "acting self," everything changes—mindset, misconceptions, and what is possible.

LORNA WING

TODAY, LORNA WING is considered by many to be an autism hero. A British psychiatrist and mother of a daughter with severe autism, she dedicated her life to unravelling the mystery of a childhood condition few people had heard of, let alone understood, when her daughter was first diagnosed around the age of three.

It was 1956 when Lorna and John Wing became parents and welcomed their daughter, Susie, into the world. They were delighted. But during the first year, they began to notice that their baby girl seemed different from other infants. Susie was a restless baby, difficult to console. As Lorna recalled, "her sucking was poor and she hardly slept at night, screaming most of the time" (2011, 178). Other times, their baby seemed withdrawn and rather passive. As Susie approached her first birthday, her mother finally became aware that something was terribly wrong. They were riding on a train, sitting opposite another mother with a little boy around the same age as Susie. As the train passed by some sheep grazing in a pasture, the little boy began to point out the window, looking to his mother to share in his excitement. Lorna suddenly realized that Susie had never shared similar moments of excitement with her, never sought out her mother's attention to experience together the wondrous sights and sounds of the world around them. Lorna would never forget how she felt that day: "A cold chill settled over me and I became very worried" (Rhodes 2011).

Later, when Susie turned three, the Wings still had no idea how to help their daughter. Nothing in their medical or psychiatric training could explain what was wrong with their little girl. Then John went to a lecture given by Mildred Creak, a pioneer in childhood psychiatry who was in the process of developing criteria for diagnosing autism. That was the day "light dawned," Lorna recalled. John realized that Creak was describing many of their daughter's own developmental challenges: "her lack of communication and social interaction, lack of pretend play and her repetitive behaviour." Finally there was a name to describe their daughter's condition: "It was obvious that Susie had classic Kanner's autism. She also had moderate to severe intellectual disabilities" (2011, 178).

As both a mother and a psychiatrist, Lorna focused all her attention on researching and learning as much as she could about this rare and poorly understood condition, switching her specialty from adult to child psychiatry. At the time, there were no supports or resources available to families, and children like Susie were often institutionalized. But John and Lorna would never allow that to happen. Lorna didn't waste any time and was determined to help not only her daughter but also other children and families who were facing a similar challenge. There was much work ahead, and Lorna Wing would not disappoint.

What follows is a sampling of Lorna Wing's many ground-breaking accomplishments along the revolutionary path she forged, broadening our understanding of autism.

1962—Founding the National Society for Autistic Children

Lorna Wing was committed to improving the quality of life for families and their children with autism and special needs. She worked with other parents to found the National Society for Autistic Children (NSAC) in London, later known as the National Autistic Society (NAS). The main goals were to set up a school for children with autism; to establish a residential program when children finish school; to provide information, resources and services; and to conduct research in partnership with parents and professionals.

1964—Establishing the Ealing School

The NSAC helped establish one of the first schools for children with autism just two years after the founding of the society. The Ealing School, in West London, was headed by the gifted teacher Sybil Elgar, whom Lorna Wing later described, in Elgar's obit-uary in the *Guardian* in 2007, as "a pioneer in the education and care of children and adults with autism." Susie, now nine years old, would become one of the first students to attend Elgar's class. Students like Susie would learn new skills in a supportive and enriching environment. Educating children with autism and special needs was a revolutionary idea at the time, but Lorna recognized early on that the right kind of education was essential for improving the lives of children with autism. The Ealing School received much attention when it opened and counted the Beatles among its supporters. Today the Ealing School, now called the Sybil Elgar School as a tribute to its gifted teacher's legacy, continues to promote the NAS mandate: "Accept difference. Not indifference."

1966—Promoting Early Intervention

The Wings were among the first to recognize and promote the importance of remedial intervention during an autistic child's early years. In 1966, John edited a collection of essays, *Early Childhood Autism: Clinical, Educational and Social Aspects*, which offered a more organic understanding of the nature of autism as part of children's biology, recognizing that, with proper early interventions, they could be helped. (Lorna edited the second edition of the book, ten years later.) The book's foreword states: "If fundamental problems are recognized early and maximum help given when it is most needed, the natural tendency towards improvement as the child matures can be fostered, the disturbed behavior managed, the family supported, and the child's disabilities minimized by skilled remedial teaching" ([1966] 1969, xi). This was in stark contrast to the prevailing "refrigerator mother" theory, which had blamed the parents for their child's autism.

This book was representative of an important change taking place in both Britain and the US, as researchers began to focus on the developmental needs of the child.

1972—Publishing *Autistic Children: A Guide for Parents*

For the first time, parents could set aside feeling helpless or at fault to embrace with confidence the vital role they could play in helping their child. The guide offered parents practical advice, ways to teach new skills, and positive methods for managing many of the challenges they were facing. But most of all, Lorna Wing gave them hope.

1970s—Developing DISCO

Lorna Wing and her colleague, psychologist Judith Gould, continued their important work through the 1970s and developed a clinical assessment interview to assist with diagnosis. The Diagnostic Interview for Social and Communication Disorders (DISCO) is widely used around the world today and is considered to be one of the most detailed forms of clinical assessment.

1972 to 1979—Undertaking the Camberwell Register Study

In 1972, Lorna Wing and Judith Gould began an ambitious study, collecting and reviewing data on children born between 1956 and 1970 and living in Camberwell, South London.

The findings from their study marked the moment when a more expansive understanding of autism began to evolve. This was a turning point, and many children would soon benefit from this revolutionary new understanding. For the first time, the narrow focus on definitions and labels could be broadened toward a more informed understanding of how to address the individual needs of the child.

Lorna continued to develop their new concept of a broad and multidimensional "autism spectrum." She explained, "The best way to look at and describe these children is on the dimensional system. You look at all the different dimensions of social skills, motor skill comprehension and use of language, etc., and describe where they are on each. That gives you a meaningful profile in terms of helping that child. You don't say he fits this or that group" (Feinstein 2010, 151).

1974—Establishing the Adult Residential Programme

Sybil Elgar and the National Society for Autistic Children—where Lorna Wing was a board member—went on to establish Somerset Court, the first residential community for adults with autism. Elgar recognized that young adults with more severe autism would need the ongoing support of a more protective community setting, along with opportunities to maintain and develop the skills they had learned at school. As an adult, Susie Wing lived with assistance in a small home for people with developmental challenges. She returned home to her parents on weekends, where they enjoyed each other's company, sharing their love of music and the joy they found in the small but important advances Susie made in her life.

1981—Introducing Asperger's Syndrome

Lorna Wing published "Asperger's Syndrome: A clinical account," in the journal *Psychological Medicine*.

1991—Founding the National Autistic Centre for Social and Communication Disorders

Lorna Wing, with Judith Gould, founded the NAS's National Autistic Centre for Social and Communication Disorders, the first resource in Britain to provide assessment and advice services for children, adolescents, and adults. Lorna worked as a part-time consultant and provided training for professionals on diagnostics. In 2008, it was renamed the Lorna Wing Centre for Autism.

2006—*What's So Special about Autism?*

Lorna Wing published a concise booklet of a mere thirty pages entitled *What's So Special about Autism?* that proved handy and helpful to many families.

2013—"Autistic Spectrum Disorder" Added to DSM-5

The American Psychiatric Association officially recognized the concept of an "autistic spectrum disorder," adding it to the DSM-5 in 2013. Lorna Wing played an active role advocating for this important change in order to better serve the needs of individuals with autism spectrum disorder.

FOLLOWING SUSIE'S death in 2005, at the age of forty-nine, Lorna Wing arranged to have her daughter's brain donated for medical research. She also arranged for a similar donation for herself and her husband. John Wing died in 2010, aged eighty-seven. Lorna continued her important work well into her eighties. She died in June 2014, aged eighty-five, but her influence lives on. Lorna Wing was always ahead of her time, and we are still trying to catch up.

BRUGHA 2011 Rhodes 2011; Gould 2014; L. Wing 2001, 2007; *Times London* 2014; Grace 2018

7

Hyperlexia and Cracking the Code

NOT ONLY HAVE I received a first-rate education from my students, but I also came to rely on many of their parents, who took me under their wing and even as I was writing this book continued to send me resources and share personal stories, providing me with a privileged and meaningful connection to what can make a difference in the lives of their children.

A few years ago, I received an email from a student's mother suggesting I read an essay in the *New York Times* by Priscilla Gilman (2013), about her son, Benj, and his precocious reading ability, known as hyperlexia. In her email, my student's mother also mentioned that the essay addressed some of the same concerns she'd had with her own son, and she thought I might find it helpful in my efforts to raise awareness about the importance of literacy education. The article was exactly what I had been looking for.

If I could choose the best description for hyperlexia, it would be Gilman's portrayal of Benj and his fascination with the written word: "Reading has been a hugely important skill that has enabled Benj to learn how to have conversations and adapt to his environment. But it has also been a passion that has sustained him on its own terms and for its own sake."[1] Gilman's words capture the spirit of what I've discovered in many of my own students who are fascinated with, or reliant on, the written word. I see hyperlexia, at the very least, as an opportunity to understand how they view and experience the world and to appreciate and respect what they value and care about. But more importantly, it demonstrates an incredible strength from which further skills, abilities, and passions can be explored and developed. Gilman's description highlights those strengths and provides a way forward to yet unrealized potential.

You can read Priscilla Gilman's essay "Early Reader" (August 25, 2013) on the *New York Times* website.

nyti.ms/13UmHFv

Yet, like many other parents and teachers like me, Gilman often encountered a very different view of hyperlexia, one more focused on deficits and problem behaviours. Gilman's account of what followed Benj's diagnosis of hyperlexia at age three reflects this deficits-based mindset, which still has a strong influence on the way literacy education is viewed today for students with ASD: "[H]e was given a diagnosis of a rare disorder called hyperlexia: the ability to read at an early age coupled with difficulty with social interaction and verbal communication, and typically, although not exclusively, found in children on the autism spectrum."

As she began to research hyperlexia and speak with professionals, the message, repeated over and over again, was that this isolated skill of reading, when accompanied by autistic tendencies, "was meaningless, mechanical, a 'splinter skill,' an ability that occurs in isolation and has no relationship to the general level of functioning or quality of life of the individual." In addition, she was told that "Benj didn't understand what he was reading and that his reading was akin to hand-flapping or running in circles—a 'self-stimulatory activity.' He reread books not because he loved them but because he 'craved sameness'... His use of a quotation to describe his experience—a fragment of a Yeats poem to depict the night sky—was 'echolalia,' mindless parroting. I was encouraged to redirect him away from reading/reciting and to think of his need to read as a problematic behavior."

Intuitively, Gilman asked how voracious reading could be anything other than "an expression of curiosity, engagement, and love." As a former assistant professor of English at Yale, who clearly shares her son's love of literature and poetry, Gilman provides a thoughtful and moving response in her 2013 *New York Times* article to the many misconceptions surrounding hyperlexia, along with hope that some educators are beginning to take a more strength-based approach:

> But I knew that Benj's reading was not merely symptomatic, and that it should not be dismissed as or reduced to a splinter skill. I took heart in the Web sites that told me I could use Benj's reading ability to help him develop appropriate behaviors, functional language and social connections. So we taught Benj proper responses to common questions by writing the questions and answers on note cards; his nursery school teachers fostered his connection to other children by having him read books to the group or pass out name tags; we handled challenging situations by writing him little stories to explain what to expect and how to cope. Characters from books helped Benj both understand and invent himself.

SPLINTER SKILLS

HYPERLEXIA AND savant expert Darold Treffert describes splinter skills as follows:

> In general there are three levels of savant ability: "splinter skills," "talented" and "prodigious"... Most common are "splinter skills," which include, for example, obsessive preoccupation with, absorption in, and memorization of, music and sports trivia, license plate numbers, maps, historical facts, birth dates, train or bus schedules, automobile makes and models, or any number of obscure preoccupations such as with vacuum cleaner motor sounds... These splinter skills are seen in as many as one in ten autistic children. (2012, 24)

He adds two caveats, though (Treffert et al. n.d., i): "The term 'splinter skill' does not mean such an ability, such as hyperlexia, is unimportant or can be disregarded. Rather, it can be an important teaching tool to support development of language and social skills."

DAROLD TREFFERT

IT WAS 1962 when Darold Treffert met his first savant. He had just completed his psychiatric residency at University Hospitals in Madison, Wisconsin, and had been asked to start a children's unit at the Winnebago Mental Health Institute near Oshkosh. The children and adolescents in the unit had severe mental handicaps, and many had been diagnosed with autism. Four patients in particular immediately caught his attention. There was a young boy who was mute and cognitively impaired but could glance at a 500-piece jigsaw puzzle, then put it together picture-side down. Another patient, an adolescent named John, was fascinated with public transit and had effortlessly memorized all of the bus routes for the city of Milwaukee. Equally impressive was the young man Treffert (2012, 2) describes as a "walking this-day-in-history almanac" who enjoyed quizzing the new doctor each morning about what important events had occurred on that day in history; even when Treffert tried to "bone up the evening before," he couldn't keep up with his patient's extraordinary memory. Another boy whom he would never forget displayed great spatial abilities and "mechanical, pitching-machine-like accuracy" by making perfect basketball free throws into the net each and every time. Yet all of these children required the care provided by the children's unit.

Treffert immediately realized that "savant skills are spectacular and worthy of our attention" and soon understood that a "teach to the talent" approach would open up new opportunities for the development of language, social, and daily living skills and more independent lives. More importantly, this approach would also offer an opportunity to learn about the person and their passions while helping them make meaningful social connections with others: "I have learned as much about matters of the heart as I have about circuits in the brain," he wrote (xiv).

At the time when he was establishing the children's unit, Treffert could find little research about autism beyond what he had learned from Leo Kanner, who first coined the term *autism* in 1944. Kanner had been a visiting professor while Treffert was still in medical school, and Kanner's teaching had ignited Treffert's lifelong interest in autism. Then, in 1964, Treffert found an invaluable resource in Bernard Rimland's book *Infantile Autism*; it would become his "compass and guide." He and Rimland began a correspondence that led to their mutual interest in autistic savant syndrome.

Today, Darold Treffert is one of the leading experts on autism and savant syndrome, which he examines in great detail in his most recent book, *Islands of Genius: The Bountiful Mind of the Autistic, Acquired, and Sudden Savant* (2010). He describes the syndrome as "a rare but remarkable condition in which incredible abilities—'islands of genius'—coexist side by side, in jarring juxtaposition, to certain disabilities within the same person" (xiii–xiv). The fiftieth-anniversary edition of *Infantile Autism* includes Treffert's update on Rimland's observations on savant syndrome.

Now in his mid-eighties, Darold Treffert continues to dedicate his life to meeting the needs of all children, spending much of his time surrounded by children at the Treffert Center Academy in Fond du Lac, Wisconsin. The students, who range in age from two and a half to twelve years, are given the opportunity to gain skills and experience in a creative and positive, inclusive environment (in preschool, junior kindergarten, after-school, and summer programming). The program's strength-based approach to learning encourages children to reach their full potential and enter primary school ready to learn. A similar approach is featured in a new, inclusive community-engaged charter school, the Treffert Way for the Exceptional Mind, which teaches students from kindergarten to sixth grade. The school models best teaching practices based on sound neurological principles.

The Treffert Center also includes the Treffert Library, Treffert's collection of savant artwork, and a clinic that supplies access to autism-based services, along with providing professional development for local public schools and hosting important international conferences. (I attended one such conference in 2018, called "Autism, Hyperlexia and Einstein Syndrome," which was the result of Treffert's ongoing "interest in children who read early [hyperlexia] or speak late [Einstein syndrome] and their relationship [or not] to autism.")

RIMLAND (1964) 2015 Treffert 2012, 1990; Treffert Center

DAROLD TREFFERT, Bernard Rimland, and Ruth Sullivan acted as consultants for the Oscar-winning film *Rain Man* (1988), raising awareness about a condition many had never heard of, let alone understood.

In the foreword to Treffert's *Hyperlexia Manual: A Guide to Children Who Read Early*, he identifies three distinct categories of hyperlexia, and clearly states the importance of hyperlexia as a teaching tool:

Type 1 are neurotypical children who simply read early. Type 2 are children who read early and the hyperlexia is a "splinter skill" along with many of the other characteristic symptoms of ASD. Type 3 are children who read early but have what I call "autistic-like" symptoms that fade over time rather than occur in more permanent ASD. As it turns out, in these cases the autism diagnosis had been mistakenly applied prematurely and inaccurately... And while the "autistic-like" features do fade over time in hyperlexia 3, that does not happen all by itself. Often those features and behaviors require the same interventions addressing the communication difficulties, sensory integration and social issues taking into account the learning style of all children with hyperlexia whether hyperlexia 2 or 3. (Treffert et al., n.d., 1–2)

The Hyperlexia Manual: A Guide to Children Who Read Early, available through the Treffert Center in Fond du Lac, Wisconsin, is an invaluable collection of practical and enriching strength-based classroom strategies and approaches founded on sound educational principles. I wish it had been available when I was teaching.

agnesian.com/services/treffert-center

"A Cover Is Not the Book"

Several of my adolescent students had taught themselves to read at an early age, but I learned of their precocious ability, and the connection between reading and speaking for them, only from their parents. I knew they loved books and writing things out, and that they responded well when I wrote things down to clarify information, but there was no mention of hyperlexia or early reading ability in their records—it was considered to be relatively insignificant so there was no need to bring it to an educator's attention. Yet this information is extremely important, as it is an indicator of strong visual skills and a passion for and interest in words. Temple

Grandin (2013, 187) describes these students as the "word-fact thinkers."

Hyperlexia offers a window into the particular learning style and strengths and abilities of our students. I noticed that my adolescent students with hyperlexia seemed to show a preference for the visual modality for processing information, as well as possessing strong auditory and visual memory. Common traits included a fascination with maps, trains, and train schedules; a heightened awareness of visual patterns and puzzles; and artistic abilities or an interest in art, architecture, or things of a mechanical nature; and the savant ability of calendaring. They also had a tendency to think in concrete and literal terms. Many relied on using dialogue or phrases from movies, television shows, or computer games, or repeated parts of conversations that they had memorized and stored in their personal language database. In addition, the students often displayed a preference for connecting with and understanding the world in visual terms—that is, they needed to first see it in order to understand it. (As Treffert wisely recommends, "If in doubt, write it out.")

HYPERLEXIA
A CLUSTER OF CHARACTERISTICS

I WAS introduced to the Canadian Hyperlexia Association by a parent; while the association is no longer active, a helpful online archive of their resource remains (judyanddavid.com/cha). This website beautifully captures some of the characteristics of hyperlexia, which will vary in presentation from child to child. Here is an abbreviated summary:

- a precocious ability to read words at a very early age, often before the child begins to talk

- an intense fascination with letters, numbers, logos, maps, or visual patterns

- significant difficulty in understanding spoken language

- rarely initiates conversations

- difficulty in socializing and interacting appropriately with people

- an intense need to keep routines, and difficulties with transitions

- specific and unusual fears

- self-stimulatory behaviour

- strong auditory and visual memory; a tendency to model the actions of others when unable to understand teacher's instructions

- difficulty answering wh— questions (who, what, when, where, why)

- thinking in concrete and literal terms

- listens selectively, appears to be deaf

- needs to see everything written down to make sense of it

- use of echolalia

- normal development until eighteen to twenty-four months, then regression

As I dug into some helpful books and resources about hyperlexia and implemented some of the suggested strategies, my students began to benefit from this strength-based approach. Many of these resources are based on a solid understanding of thinking patterns and learning styles, but also include the added perspective of gifted speech and language pathologists. The resource material by Phyllis Kupperman was extremely useful. She is a renowned speech and language pathologist and founder and executive director of the Center for Speech and Language Disorders in Elmhurst and Chicago, Illinois. Kupperman has a unique understanding of how to develop communication and learning skills for children of all ages and levels of ability, along with extensive experience in working with hyperlexia as a tool for building language skills for children with ASD.

A wonderful resource by Phyllis Kupperman is *The Source: Intervention in Autism Spectrum Disorders* (2nd ed.).

Nurturing the Spark

The mother who directed me to the Gilman essay included her own account of her son's early fascination with letters and the extraordinary impact this had on his development—for it was through reading that he learned to talk. In her email she writes:

> When he was 2ish and not talking (first word at 26 months), his grandmother... bought him a plastic placemat with the alphabet and pictures all around the edge. He liked the letters, not the pictures as much. And he learned what the letters and sounds were quite easily. I then bought him plastic letters that stuck on the side of the bathtub. He was about 3. I would sit with him at bath time and stick up 2 or

3 letter words and he would make the sound of each letter and then put them together and say the words. So, he read at 3 also. That is how he learned to talk, reading first. So, he was hyperlexic and thank God for it.

An amazing feat for a child of "2ish" with communication and sensory challenges: he learned to read as a way to discover his words and develop the ability to speak. It was reading that brought his words to life as he began to unlock the elusive code of language hidden within his precious plastic alphabet letters. This marvellous connection between hyperlexia and language acquisition provides a wonderful opportunity not only to understand neuroplasticity and the brain's adaptability but also to unlock the great potential that such exceptional skills provide.

Another student, Kenny, whom you'll hear more about later, also learned to speak through reading. When I was searching for hyperlexia resources, Kenny's mother suggested I visit Parentbooks, in Toronto, to find more helpful resources on hyperlexia. The knowledgeable staff there suggested I read *The Spark: A Mother's Story of Nurturing Genius*, by Kristine Barnett (2013), about her extraordinary son Jake, who was diagnosed with autism as a toddler. With the help and determination of his mother, Jake's true potential was nurtured and developed, as described in Barnett's moving account of their journey.

Jake could sound out the words *cat* and *dog* and had taught himself the alphabet before he could walk. At around fourteen months, he began to show signs of regression, speaking less and less. But he remained fascinated with his alphabet letters and cards. Well-intentioned special educators told Barnett to remove her son's alphabet cards before sending him off to preschool each morning, as they felt his "obsession" with the cards prevented him from learning. They failed to recognize the value of Jake's interest in the alphabet and, in keeping with the deficit mindset, believed that since he would never be able to speak or read, the cards were meaningless and served no purpose. But Barnett intuitively questioned this recommendation, removed Jake from the school, and set up her own pre-kindergarten daycare program for Jake and other neighbourhood children, including children with autism, called Little Light:

> What if carrying around alphabet cards everywhere he goes is Jake's way of saying he wants to read? Maybe it's not but what if it is? Do we want him with people who won't even try to teach him simply because it's not part of the life skills program? Why would they say no to somebody who wants to learn?... Why is it all about what these kids can't do? Why isn't anyone looking more closely at what they can do... He was so special, so unique. But he was also autistic, and just because of that, his school had labeled him and then prematurely decided what he could and couldn't do. He needed me to be his advocate, his champion... So instead of hammering away at all the tasks these kids couldn't do, I thought we'd start with what they wanted to do. This approach was far from standard practice... We met the children where they were in order to get them where they needed to be. (2013, 56–77)

Now Jake would be able to keep his precious cards close at hand. His speech did return, along with a passion for reading and "thinking." Jake Barnett followed his "spark" and was accepted at the age of eleven as a student at Indiana University–Purdue University Indianapolis, where he spent four years studying mathematics and physics. He was then accepted, at the age of fifteen, at the Perimeter Institute for Theoretical Physics in Waterloo, Ontario (Wells 2013).

While Jake is clearly exceptional, it is important to recognize that his extraordinary abilities might have remained unrealized had his mother not chosen to follow the more unconventional path of nurturing her son's strengths and illuminating his "spark."

Now a young adult, Jake waxes eloquent on the importance of "thinking." You can hear him tell his inspiring story in his TEDx talk and in an interview on TVO.

youtube.com/ watch?v=Uq-FOO-Q1TpEtvo.org/video/ programs/the-agen- da-with-steve-paikin/ tapping-the-potential

Gilman, Treffert, Barnett, my students, and their parents provided the thoughtful and caring viewpoint I was looking for, portraying hyperlexia as an important skill that should no longer be ignored or dismissed but, rather, considered and understood as a strength and opportunity to gain a deeper appreciation of such extraordinary abilities. Perhaps now we might begin to see a shift in mindset as we consider looking beyond exceptional skills toward the wondrous potential within.

Islands of Genius

Darold Treffert's award-winning book, *Islands of Genius: The Bountiful Mind of the Autistic, Acquired, and Sudden Savant*, presents savant syndrome as proof of the brain's plasticity, and points to the value the study of savant syndrome has for all of us:

> [A] rare but remarkable condition in which incredible abilities—"islands of genius"—coexist side by side, in jarring juxtaposition, to certain disabilities within the same person... [N]ew findings have demonstrated that the brain

is a much more malleable structure throughout life…
Savant syndrome provides convincing proof of brain plasticity—the capacity of the brain to rewire and restructure
itself after damage whether by genetic, injury or illness
process. And with brain plasticity comes a much more
optimistic view of the central nervous system's capacity to
repair and restore itself, and all the enormous implications
and positive ramifications such a view entails in the rapidly
expanding field of neuroscience. (2012, xiii–xiv, xviii)

In his contribution to the fiftieth-anniversary edition of
Bernard Rimland's seminal work, *Infantile Autism* (2014,
242-43), Treffert provides many interesting and important
facts about savant syndrome. Here is an abbreviated summary of some of the key points.

- Savant syndrome can be understood as a neurological
  recruitment and rewiring of undamaged brain capacity
  (neuroplasticity) in response to dysfunction or injury.

- Savant syndrome appears in about 1 in 10 persons with
  autism. "[N]ot all savants are autistic, and not all persons
  with autism are savants."

- Male savants outnumber females by a range of between
  four and six to one.

- IQ in savants can range from subnormal to exceptional.

- "The special skills and abilities in autism are generally
  in music, art, calendar calculating, lightning calculating,
  and mechanical/spatial areas … Whatever the special skill,
  it is always linked to massive memory within the area of
  that skill."

- "The special savant skill is most often in a single area, but multiple skills can exist in some savants."

- "Savant skills are not frivolous. Rather, by 'training the talent' there is an accompanying increase in language, social, and daily living skills as a conduit toward independence."

- Vivid recall can be "sensational," but "the savant can be creative."

- All savants show that they "know things they never learned."

- "While most often savant syndrome is evident from birth or early childhood (congenital), in some cases savant abilities suddenly and unexpectedly surface in some adolescents or adults following head injury, strokes, or other central nervous system disorder (acquired). This hints at dormant potential—a little *Rain Man* perhaps—within us all."

THE BLETCHLEY "ENIGMA" CODE CRACKERS

HYPERLEXIA BRINGS to mind the clever Bletchley code crackers of WWII, headed by Alan Turing. Today it is believed that Turing, and many members of his group, may themselves have fallen somewhere along the spectrum and had their share of "splinter skills," having privileged access to the brain's ability to decipher codes and make rapid calculations. Their unique processing abilities and exceptional skill set made it possible for them to decipher the ever-changing German "Enigma" code, hastening the end of the war and thereby saving many lives.

Turing is also credited with creating the concept and prototype for today's computers, and rumours suggest that the famous Apple computer logo, an apple with a bite out of it, may be a respectful nod from Steve Jobs to Turing, whom he greatly admired. The appalling way Turing was treated after the war, when he was exposed and charged as a homosexual, caused him to take his own life by biting into an apple laced with cyanide; the apple was found on his nightstand, beside his body.

Turing's tragic death should serve as a harsh reminder about how much can be lost when people are viewed as different and then discounted and made expendable or punished. We are all beholden to the Bletchley code crackers, a group of people who "marched to their own drummer," and their accomplishments and uniqueness should serve to remind us of the value of being different and how much we all need each other.[2]

Rethinking Hyperlexia

So how might we think about a skill like hyperlexia from a more psycholinguistic and neuroplastic perspective, rather than from a purely behavioural perspective? In the early 1970s, as a more neurological understanding of learning disabilities began to unfold, a meaningful and necessary partnership was formed with psycholinguistics, described by Dictionary.com as "the study of the relationship between language and the cognitive or behavioral characteristics of those who use it." Books like Frank Smith's *Understanding Reading: A Psycholinguistic Analysis of Reading and Learning to Read* (1971) were at the forefront of this new understanding.

Smith, a pioneer in the field of psycholinguistics, described his interest in this subject as "the intricate and fascinating and beautiful human quality—'skill' is really too cold a word— of language... I began by using reading as a way to study language and ended up using language as one of the ways in which to understand reading" (ix).

In typical development, children naturally and intuitively learn to speak by verbalizing and repeating sounds they hear as they move through the well-known stages of language acquisition. This typical developmental pathway is what many people have come to expect and therefore believe is the correct and only way to acquire language.

Spoken words and conversational exchanges can be fleeting and difficult to grasp. When faced with the challenges of processing what they hear, some children have discovered that they can rely more on their visual abilities in their determined effort to crack the code of language. A more difficult path, certainly, but it is precisely that determined effort that tells us how much they want to communicate with us and figure out what we are saying. Shouldn't we at least do the same in return?

It appears that in their early years, some children with delayed speech or regression and autistic tendencies may learn to rely more on their visual strengths as a way of compensating for their sensory integration difficulties. As their ability to process information in the visual modality increases through constant practice and repetition (perseveration), letters that can be seen, touched, and controlled can now be matched to sounds. Over time, the auditory and the visual can be perceived as a single, unified, and integrated sensory experience (percept)—something that eluded them without the help of their alphabet letters. By first accessing the world of "sound" through visual letters, words, and books, understanding spoken language, despite its fast pace, is suddenly brought into reach for these children, slowed down and captured and held in the palm of their hand to be studied, processed, decoded, repeated, rehearsed, and internalized, all in their own time and on their own terms. Repetition and the need for sameness may be important aspects of the learning process, necessary for their unique style of acquiring language. Maria Montessori noted such repetitive behaviours as an important aspect of learning; care must be taken so as not to confuse developmental delays and behaviours with pathology.

The visual pathway may enable the children to more easily control, practice, and rehearse letters and sounds in their own time frame in order to eventually internalize them when they finally begin to speak.

In other words, reading may provide an alternate accessible pathway by which some children begin to acquire language skills. The children appear to have cleverly directed their focus away from the busy, noisy sensory world of verbal exchanges toward their preference for the quiet constancy of visual written letters—they may "retreat" into themselves in order to find a safe and quiet haven in which to focus and concentrate on the written word, and thereby crack the language "code" as slowly as they need to. Here, time stands still long enough for them to figure it out.

It may seem counterintuitive to imagine that reading can develop before speaking. For typical people, it might seem strange and almost impossible for children to teach themselves how to read, let alone learn how to speak from reading, while at the same time struggling to follow or understand what a person is saying. Many would likely but erroneously conclude that if children can't understand what is said to them, then they most likely can't understand what they are reading. But such is the paradoxical nature of ASD.

Typical children babble and continually make sounds, which they repeat over and over again, and we enthusiastically reward this repetition. Similarly, children with hyperlexia must rehearse their written letters and words over and over again, as sounds and symbols are codified through practice. The repetitive behaviour may appear more extreme simply because it is different from what we are used to observing in typical development. But the children begin to discover linguistic patterns as they repetitively "play" with their plastic letters or cards or repeatedly read their favourite books. Learning to speak by following the reading road to language naturally takes greater effort and much practice. As the children begin to load up their memory with an extensive database of words and expressions, it is not unusual to see the emergence of speech along with another characteristic, called echolalia, as they advance toward the next level (scaffold) of language integration and acquisition.

The precocious nature of this ability to read before speaking often results in advanced decoding skills, which may in turn result in an extraordinary ability to read material far above a child's level of maturity and comprehension. But it does not follow that they cannot comprehend anything at all simply because their decoding skills naturally outpace their life experiences.

It is extremely important that we understand and respect this atypical schedule of milestones in our efforts to design effective therapies, before dismissing them altogether, as we come to accept and recognize that there are different yet equally valuable pathways toward cracking the language code. The children's resourcefulness is astounding, and their compensatory/adaptive strategies have much to teach us in our efforts to better serve their needs. Their unique ability opens up a whole world of communication for these children, a world that might otherwise have eluded them. Insignificant and meaningless? I think not, for it would seem to follow that unique and different minds take unique and different developmental pathways, and if we go down those pathways together, we just might discover many more strengths and abilities along the way, and at the same time address the challenges that naturally result when square pegs encounter round holes.

As a teacher, I still can't believe that a strength or skill such as reading could possibly be viewed as a meaningless and problematic behaviour. This behavioural interpretation would seem to point to the lingering influence of the old understanding of ASD and shows a strong resistance to the acceptance of ASD in true neurological terms. It seems this acceptance has gone only as far as serving as an explanation of ASD as a "condition," without embracing the neurological effect on the "thinking self" in all its forms and aspects. Within such a limited view, no further investigation or thought is deemed necessary—a focus on "the acting self" and "what's wrong" limits the need to consider the neurological implications for treatment and education.

As educators we know that all "learning and mislearning is neurological" (Cruikshank 1980). Yet even in the face of what we know as educators, along with the important research that addresses the neurological learning implications of ASD, this mindset has been slow to embrace important opportunities for exploring learning potential. It seems that more effort and resources are still being devoted to seeking a "cure" for ASD, rather than exploring the learning potential of traits of unique minds.

Working with Autism, Not against It

Given what we now know about the brain and autism, do we still want to see hyperlexia as simply a meaningless and insignificant mechanical skill rather than as a neuroplastic detour along a road less travelled toward cracking the language code?

The brain works in mysterious ways, and there is much we need to learn. We must also proceed with caution before imposing a typical pattern of development on unique minds. Again, the concept of "working with autism, not against it" must be foremost in our quest to bridge the gap that divides us. It is precisely the brain's ability to adapt to challenges that offers so much hope and promise. But it requires a great deal of change on our part, too; we must recognize that the road less travelled, while challenging, can still hold the promise of a worthwhile journey. I've been on that road with my students, as they found their own way, and then met them at the crossroads, each of us then a little more aware of the other and just a little bit wiser.

8

Echolalia and Thinking in Scripts

E VERYONE LOVES TO use favourite lines from popular or classic movies: "Here's lookin' at you, kid"; "ET phone home"; "May the force be with you"; "Live long and prosper"; "There's no place like home." I'm sure you can identify the movie and speaker in each without much effort. These famous lines have become part of our daily conversational exchanges and are often used to emphasize a particular idea or feeling, as well as create a sense of familiarity and connection. They are like literary or poetic devices, making allusions to familiar pop culture references that capture the essence of what we are trying to say. It really is a great way to spice up our conversations.

Some people with ASD develop a fascination with particular movies or TV shows and memorize much of the dialogue. Many of my students quoted extensively from movie and TV scripts, and even those who did not have this trait thought it was cool and joined in. This tendency to use borrowed dialogue was a common characteristic among my students with hyperlexia; it seemed to be a natural progression from the constancy of the written word toward the constancy of the spoken word, stored as dialogue, to be imported and used to fit the situation or context. Spontaneous speech, on the other hand, was far more challenging; dialogue from favourite scripts could serve as a substitute when finding the right words was just too daunting.

Marc: "And Me without My Camera"

One of the best compliments I have ever received was from a student who loved *The Simpsons*. I had an important meeting at school that day, so I arrived in the morning wearing a nice dress with a lovely batik scarf, instead of my more casual, everyday look. I really didn't think my students would take much notice, but as I entered the class, Marc immediately ran over to me and, in his best Bart Simpson voice, said, "And me without my camera." A better compliment I couldn't imagine. It still makes me smile and blush a little even as I write about it.

Now, this exchange on its own may not seem that unusual, but keep in mind that this same student had a great deal of difficulty participating in the more traditional prosaic and spontaneous conversational exchanges of daily life, the sort of exchanges most people take for granted. Instead, Marc frequently relied on his cherished "scripts" to express himself and often had difficulty finding his own "voice" and spontaneous words. Many professionals in the field of ASD refer to this style of speaking as echolalia. And many still view it as a meaningless parroting behaviour that should be discouraged. But the research presents a very different understanding of this trait.

Conversational exchanges require quick responses and improvisation. For most people, such exchanges happen quite naturally and spontaneously, a daily occurrence that we find neither onerous nor challenging.

Yet, we marvel at jazz musicians who can create original and immediate musical responses and improvise in the moment, a skill that eludes many classically trained musicians. Imagine a classically trained musician, reliant on sheet music and following the conductor's lead, suddenly asked to "Take it!" and play a jazz riff to Beethoven's Ninth; this would certainly present a daunting challenge to even the most experienced classical musician. For many people with ASD, the spontaneous and improvisational nature of conversational exchanges in daily life demands skills not unlike those of jazz musicians.

I believe my students who sometimes relied on "scripts" and borrowed dialogue used their personal databases of memorized scripts to keep pace with the rhythm of language and to quickly fill the silences that might otherwise have brought conversations to an abrupt end. Their method and style of engagement may have appeared rather unconventional, but the desire to connect with others and communicate was nevertheless strong and sincere, and their unique method of communicating was often delivered with confidence, good humour, and a sense of accomplishment. They seemed pleased when they found the right quote to match the situation. "And me without my camera" was a perfect match, wouldn't you agree?

Although many of these students had well-developed vocabularies and verbal abilities, they still found themselves at a loss for words during more prosaic and fact-based exchanges. (I encountered many students over the years with similar learning profiles, who also spoke and understood several other languages.) At such times, their style remained short and to the point. However, when they wished to express a feeling or talk about a passionate interest, their style became more animated and was often peppered with borrowed dialogue. And when they wished to participate and be part of the action in the classroom, they quickly found a fitting phrase to match the situation as a way to join in. My other students who did not share this trait willingly followed suit and would play the "speaking in scripts" game as a starting point for mutual connection. The scripts seemed to provide a way for the students to break the ice, since initiating conversations in more conventional ways presented a more daunting prospect.

In more stressful situations, I also noticed a tendency toward the use of immediate echolalia—that is, repeating or "echoing" what is just heard. Their repetition of what they heard would become more pronounced and repetitive, not unlike what individuals who stutter experience. But instead of a letter or syllable being repeated, as is the case with stuttering, entire phrases would get caught up in a loop of repetition from which they seemed to have difficulty breaking free. We understand the stutterers' challenge and do not regard this trait as odd or meaningless, but do we extend the same understanding to individuals with ASD? While at times we may have difficulty comprehending what they are trying to say, there is no mistaking the meaning behind their words: their anxiety. For me, that came through loud and clear as I observed my students' struggles with expressive communication.

Many of my students, including Marc, attended a weekly community centre "dinner and dance" program with other young adults. I was curious to see what my students were like outside of the school setting; I thought it might give me the opportunity to broaden my perspective and deepen my understanding of their lives beyond the classroom walls. So, one evening, I went along to observe.

The dance instructor routinely began the evening program by asking all the participants to form a circle and introduce themselves. Newcomers were asked to go first. I noticed that Marc was becoming rather anxious as his turn to introduce himself to the group approached. Marc was uncomfortable in large group settings, and although he had participated in the introductory circle before, he was beginning to show signs of stress and anxiety. Larry, his good friend and classmate, was standing right beside him and, when it was his turn, said with confidence, "Hi, my name is Larry." Marc knew that he was next, and he began to frantically pull on the threads of his shirt. Then, he yelled, "Hi, my name is Larry."

Now, Marc was very capable of introducing himself correctly, and of course he knew his own name, but under pressure, like a deer caught in the headlights, he resorted to an old "behaviour," long since outgrown, of repeating what he had just heard. Over the years, I noticed that many of my adolescent students with ASD sometimes fell back on old childhood strategies or behaviours that were no longer in evidence but suddenly resurfaced as a way of coping with new and unfamiliar situations. This is a very natural human reaction we've all experienced in one form or another. Old habits die hard.

The tendency to copy others when under pressure is not as unusual as it may seem. Marc's experience at the community centre immediately reminded me of a scene from *Monty Python and the Holy Grail*, in which we find the Knights of the Round Table preparing to cross the Bridge of Death, with each knight required to answer three questions before being allowed safe passage, including, "What's your favourite colour?"

I don't want to give too much away, in case you haven't viewed the scene, but we find ourselves laughing at the knights as they try to answer "the questions three," for we recognize ourselves and can appreciate why the knights who are awaiting their turn pay extra-close attention to the correct answers already offered by Lancelot, who was allowed to safely cross the bridge. Everyone, at one time or another, has relied on copying what they've overheard in order to get out of a tricky situation, to process what has been said, or to buy time as they try to think of an answer. But in this scene, copying what is heard actually proves fatal.

I love this sketch, especially the clever bit at the very end, for it not only pokes fun at this normal aspect of human nature, but also goes further, providing us with an even deeper appreciation for King Arthur's special interests and attention to facts and details. King Arthur, as portrayed by the Monty Python actor, is what Temple Grandin (2013, 187) would call a "word-fact thinker," and his special interests result in a surprising and triumphant outcome. By highlighting the value and benefits of King Arthur's special interests and attention to fine detail and facts, the scene allows us to laugh and then pause and appreciate the extraordinary nature of individuals with keen interests and passions.

You can view the "Bridge of Death" scene, and have a good laugh along with a good dose of insight, on YouTube. Perhaps King Arthur and his knights belong somewhere along the spectrum. I'd like to think so.

youtube.com/watch?v=Wpx6xnankz8

An Anthropologist on Mars

Both anxiety and stress play a significant role in the lives of individuals with ASD. Temple Grandin (1995, 259) described herself to Oliver Sacks as often feeling like "an anthropologist on Mars." Seeing oneself as an outsider, having to constantly figure out the "strange" customs and practices and unwritten rules of society, so obvious to many yet elusive to others, understandably can create a great deal of anxiety and stress for individuals with ASD. Grandin's perceptive and clever description of herself points to a thoughtful self-awareness and strong sense of self (something that many believe eludes individuals on the spectrum). We immediately understand how she sees the world and can now empathize with her experience. No doubt we neurotypicals are confounding and contradictory, not always saying what we mean or meaning what we say. How frustrating it must be to constantly have to figure out our strange ways.

A recent survey conducted by the UK's Research Autism (2016) found that "stress is the single biggest factor affecting quality of life for autistic people and their families, causing significant impact across all key aspects of life including school, work, health, relationships and behaviour."

By chance, I once had the opportunity to experience what might happen if stress could be alleviated, if only momentarily. My students always surprised me with newfound skills and abilities. While sitting in my office at school after the students had left for the day, I answered my phone and immediately recognized the unmistakable voice of Marc.

"Hello there," he said, mimicking Bart Simpson.

I started to respond, but before I could complete my sentence there was a *click* as he promptly hung up the phone. I felt quite flattered that he had taken the trouble to track me down just to say hello. I had seen him at the end of the school day and never imagined my students would give me a second thought outside of the classroom—out of sight, out of mind—so this was a pleasant surprise.

Marc delivered his telephone greeting with the economy of an old-fashioned telegram—short, to the point, message delivered, *stop*. No idle chit-chat, no need for conversation, no need for me to respond—just a short and direct message to make contact and then *click*, end of call. The telephone seemed to offer him a little more control, unlike face-to-face conversations, which tend to be more unpredictable and open-ended, with no *click* option in sight.

Marc enjoyed our new form of communication, and his after-school calls began to increase in frequency, if not duration. He often delivered greetings using a variety of voices from his favourite actors and movie characters, and I never knew who would greet me when I lifted the receiver.

One day, as I was checking my answering machine, I was surprised to discover that Marc had left me a voice message. This was a first, and I wondered which voice might greet me as I played back his message. I wasn't quite prepared for what I heard: he had actually used his own voice, with just a hint of influence from his beloved characters.

The message began, "Hi there. How are you? This is Marc..." He continued in this fashion before finishing with a proper farewell ending, rather than with an abrupt *click*. The message itself was clear and articulate, longer in duration than our earlier exchanges on the phone, and much different from his usual style of speaking in scripts. His clarity of thought and prosaic delivery shocked me, as I had not realized that he had the ability to express himself in such a thoughtful, straightforward, and determined fashion. For the first time, he used his own voice and his name rather than relying on the characters who often spoke for him. This message, and others that followed, offered a special glimpse of what is possible when anxiety levels are significantly reduced.

While most people, myself included, feel a little anxious and self-conscious when leaving a recorded phone message, in case we say the wrong thing, the opposite seemed to be true for Marc. With the anxiety he experienced during conversational exchanges now removed, the answering machine offered him uninterrupted time to express himself, along with the advantage of not having to actually speak to me in person. Leaving a message on an answering machine guaranteed Marc would not be interrupted and could deliver his monologue in peace.

The answering machine gave Marc complete control. Originally, if I answered the phone when he called, his greeting was short, but if I let the machine pick up, a far more meaningful message would be delivered. Over time, Marc became more comfortable actually talking with me on the phone about the latest events in his life, and our conversations lasted several minutes. Most striking of all was his desire to maintain a connection.

Today Marc lives in a small town with a supportive community, where everyone knows each other. He lives in his own apartment in a duplex with other family members and volunteers every day at the local food bank. He enjoys walking around town and spending time at a popular doughnut shop.

"A Different Way of Seeing Autism"

Following my instincts, I began to research echolalia on my own and soon discovered the treasure trove of work by Barry Prizant. His research on echolalia dates back to 1979, and his most recent book, *Uniquely Human: A Different Way of Seeing Autism*, published in 2015, continues to demonstrate the ongoing need to set aside the deficits view of autism toward a strength-based understanding, some forty years since first presenting this view. His research and salient findings help us understand echolalia as an important part of language development for children with ASD.

Prizant presents a more psycholinguistically based understanding of echolalia, recognizing this trait as an important and unique aspect of language development for people on the autistic spectrum. He advocates for a more educationally sound approach to fostering meaningful growth and development, based on "a different way of seeing autism":

> One reason I wanted to study echolalia was that many of the judgments about children with autism had been made by people who were not experts in speech and language or in child development. They were behavior therapists, specialists in developing programs to reduce undesirable behavior and increase desirable behavior. Most shared the belief that echolalia was in the "undesirable" category of behavior without really understanding it. (2015, 40)

In a *Huffington Post* interview with Elaine Hall—mother of an adult son with autism, founder of the Miracle Project, and author of *Seven Keys to Unlock Autism*—Prizant described his unique approach to autism and the background that led him to a lifetime of work in the autism world:

> With my training in developmental psycholinguistics, I began to question the credibility of what I read in the autism literature, especially regarding "deviant" language and so-called "aberrant behavior" in autism.
>
> In the 1970s I developed a specific interest in echolalia, the tendency for people with autism to repeat what they've heard either immediately, or at a significantly later time. Then, echolalia was described as "meaningless parroting" and "psychotic speech," and efforts were made to discourage or even punish children. My clinical work convinced

me that these children were learning to communicate through echolalia, and it was part of their unique process of language development. Their parents shared the same perceptions! I then studied four children for over a year. Through meticulous video analysis of echolalia, I proved that echolalia often was functional communication, directly contradicting prevailing behavioral views.

Research at this time was focused on documenting how different and "deviant" persons with autism were, and in 1983, I published an article arguing against this "deficits-checklist" approach to autism that dominated the field. Since then, I have focused my efforts on speaking out against harmful and inaccurate beliefs about persons with autism in our research and scholarly publications and presentations. (Hall 2015)

You can read the entire 2015 interview with Barry Prizant online at the *Huffington Post* website. You can also find Prizant's research papers on echolalia on his own website.

huffpost.com/entry/ heroes-among-us-dr- barry_b_7923008; barryprizant.com

It's hard to believe that there has been such a delay in accepting and using a true developmental understanding of autism. After forty years of solid research by Barry Prizant, Adriana Schuler, Pat Rydell, Judith Duchan, and others, professionals in the educational system and in the field of ASD still struggle to move past echolalia's behavioural presentation, toward a more cognitive and psycholinguistic understanding and the opportunities that such an understanding can offer children. Dr. Prizant's important insights were never part of the in-service training I received; instead, teachers were encouraged to try to eliminate and discourage echolalia, with no appreciation for what lay behind it. Once again, the prevailing culture of focusing on deficits, and of changing behaviour without understanding it, does not allow for the important strength-based approach that explains behaviours, and continues to resist the neurological research that would enhance it. Although Prizant wrote about echolalia as far back as the late 1970s, he still recognizes the pressing need to address this ongoing oversight.

BARRY PRIZANT

BARRY PRIZANT is considered to be a leading authority on autism, with over forty years of experience as a scholar, researcher, clinician, educator, international consultant, and autism advocate. He is co-author of *The SCERTS Model: A Comprehensive Educational Approach for Children with Autism Spectrum Disorders* (2005). The SCERTS (Social Communication, Emotional Regulation, and Transactional Support) model, used by many school districts across the US and more than a dozen countries around the world, is a strength-based approach to learning in which families, educators, and therapists work together as part of a team to help realize its full benefits.

Yet with all his accomplishments in this field, Prizant continues to see a pressing need to continue advocating on behalf of children with autism in order to overcome the outdated deficits-based view of individuals on the spectrum, still held by many educators and professionals, who in turn influence families. Both the title and subtitle of his recent book, *Uniquely Human: A Different Way of Seeing Autism* (2015), capture his important message. It seems the prevailing deficits-based culture has allowed little room for implementing a strength-based approach to autism, with its nuanced neurological and developmental understanding of autism's behavioural characteristics—the approach he has been promoting since he first became interested in autism, back in 1975.

Shortly after completing his master's degree in speech and language pathology, Prizant was assigned to work at the Buffalo Children's Hospital Autism Program as part of his clinical fellowship. He began working as a speech and language specialist in a classroom with five young boys with autism. His responsibilities included "conducting a pilot study, observing these boys to try to understand what role echolalia played in their communication and language development" (2015, 40). Echolalia is the tendency to repeat or *echo* words, phrases, expressions, or even whole sentences, often in a repetitive pattern. Prizant soon realized that echolalia served a meaningful purpose for the boys and was not a "meaningless parroting" behaviour, as was commonly believed.

Prizant has continued to work toward establishing a major shift in the way autism is understood, by reframing "behaviours" like echolalia more as compensatory strategies or a way of coping when overwhelmed by sensory information. His work demonstrates that by building on an individual's strengths and working with rather than against their compensatory strategies, new skills, abilities, and more desirable behaviours can result, while the individual's unique and special abilities are still respected. In fact, Prizant cautions that professionals who try to eliminate such behaviours or traits and try to "fix" the child may in fact interfere with the child's developmental process. He promotes a more psycholinguistically based understanding of echolalia, recognizing this trait as an important and unique aspect of language development for children on the autistic spectrum.

Uniquely Human has earned the praise of leaders in the field, including Temple Grandin, whose gold seal of approval appears on the book's cover, with the words, "I love his approach." Prizant is also greatly appreciated by many of the families he has known over the years. Elaine Hall, a well-known autism advocate, regards Prizant as her mentor, having met him when her son was first diagnosed with autism. At the conclusion of her 2015 *Huffington Post* interview with Prizant, she asked him to explain what had led him to dedicate his lifelong career to autism and to write his book. He responded, "*Uniquely Human* is my effort to bring our work to a broader audience to rectify harmful and inaccurate assumptions that have existed for too many years."

PRIZANT 2015 Hall 2015

"Here's Lookin' at You, Kid"

In spite of all the research, teachers are often told to discourage students from using echolalia or copying dialogue, since this is viewed as an inappropriate and meaningless behaviour. At times, my students were reprimanded and told to be quiet, and if the behaviour continued, they would be removed from favourite school events. I tried to explain the reasons behind my students' use of scripts and delayed echolalia, and the work of Prizant, but to no avail. Teachers, too, were beginning to lose their voice with the public education system's greater reliance on the "expertise" of outside professionals. When it came to autism, the professional voice of the teacher was no longer considered valid.

One incident in particular still makes me cringe when I recall what took place. On that day, Marc returned to class after being reprimanded by senior staff members about his use of "scripting" (echolalia). Looking rather defeated, he sat down at his desk with his head and shoulders slumped forward. He remained unusually quiet and then began to rock back and forth, a behaviour from his early years, now rarely evident and certainly never seen in class before. The other students immediately sensed their classmate's need to be left alone and kept their distance.

Later that afternoon, our class joined the rest of the school for a much-anticipated excursion. Staff and students boarded a chartered bus for the occasion and excitedly took their seats. Marc insisted on sitting beside me and as soon as we started on our way, he began repeating in a very loud voice, "Mrs. Levitt is not a professional, Mrs. Levitt is not a professional!"— over and over again for the entire bus to hear. Everyone went silent as Marc continued his chant. No one stopped him. Everyone remained uncomfortably quiet, recognizing that his chant echoed what he had heard during his reprimand earlier in the day; his words were no longer considered a meaningless phrase, for their meaning came through loud and clear. You could feel the tension and embarrassment in the air; a harder, yet more poignant, lesson, I could not imagine. If anyone still viewed echolalia as meaningless, their view quickly changed. Marc had made his point far better than my earlier attempts at presenting a different understanding of his use of echolalia. From that day forward, this sensitive, articulate, and perceptive student was never discouraged from expressing himself again. Here's lookin' at you, kid.

My students not only understood everything they heard, they would also often repeat snippets from overheard conversations. While many assume that our students are not paying attention to what is being discussed around them, they soon discover the folly of such assumptions. It never ceases to amaze me how many times professionals and educators make negative comments about students, teachers, or even parents when the student is right in front of them. Do they really believe the students don't understand what is being said or can't recognize what can be conveyed by tone of voice and or level of intensity? Unfortunately, some educators and professionals remain uninformed and hold on to such hurtful misconceptions. A lack of appreciation for our students' ability to communicate, and to understand what they hear, reflects how our students are still regarded. This saddens me, but then I remember how things changed back in the 1980s for students with learning disabilities, now appropriately referred to as students who learn differently; I remember students like Anthony, the ninth grader whose story I described at the beginning of this book, and I know things can change for the better. But the change must first begin with us.

WHEN WORDS FALL ON DEAF EARS

THE DOCUMENTARY *Life Animated* is about an outgoing young man named Owen Suskind and how his passion for Disney movies helped him discover and "write" his own animated life story. Owen began to show signs of regression at age three, but eventually found his way back with the help of his family and his memorized dialogue from his beloved Disney characters. He was also hyperlexic, and had used the credits at the end of the movies to teach himself how to read. Now that can't be easy.

Owen's father, Ron Suskind (2014), recognized that not only could he reach his son through Disney characters, he could also use them as a teaching tool: "He's turning these movies into tools that, more and more, he's using to make sense of the wider world." Sadly, these were Ron's words as he pleaded with the director of the private school Owen loved, when he was told his son could no longer remain there. Ron asked the director to please reconsider her decision but was told, "Many of these kids are just too hard to teach. Look, not picking up social cues is just too great a burden. They can't engage with teachers or peers with enough ease, enough capacity, to push themselves forward."

Thankfully, like the other parents I've mentioned, Ron followed his instinct and found the "spark" that ignited his son's potential.

Finding a New Path

When language acquisition is impeded or delayed or language disappears entirely, it seems that some children on the spectrum are able to adapt and discover a different developmental pathway, one more suited to their unique strengths and abilities. These new pathways may help children find their way back to what was lost, or provide a different and unique opportunity to develop their skills and abilities.

Hyperlexia, echolalia, lip reading (see chapter 10), and other adaptive learning strategies may provide some children with a way to adapt to sensory challenges and to develop new skills and abilities that may improve their ability to communicate. With our understanding, support, and educational expertise, we might begin to lessen their levels of anxiety and provide opportunities to develop their skills. Most importantly, by recognizing the nature of different patterns of thinking and the function of adaptive strategies, as we finally did with children with learning disabilities, we can begin to emphasize strengths rather than deficits, develop appropriate skills, improve adaptive strategies, and extend our expectations for success. But first we must recognize that education offers an important opportunity for growth and development.

The experiences of my students and of families like the Gilmans, Barnetts, Suskinds, and countless others all deserve our full attention. All of these families believed in their children and saw their "spark" when others did not. They continued to work with their children's strengths and abilities, offering us important lessons to consider very carefully.

Both the Gilman and Suskind families have rich literary backgrounds, so is it any wonder that their children found a connection through a heightened fascination with words? Benj Gilman found his way through his love of poetry and the ongoing support of his mother, who recognized early on the true heart and soul of a poet. Owen Suskind discovered that Disney was a good place to start to find his way back; in his 2014 *New York Times* article, his father, Ron Suskind, said "he wanted to connect, to feel his life fully, and using his movies and improvised tool kit we helped him build he's finding his footing." And Jake Barnett held tight to his precious alphabet cards and, with the help of his mother, was able to rediscover his voice. My students, their families, and their achievements continue to fill me with wonder.

So, what are the implications of echolalia in younger children? What happens when an overreliance on "scripts" makes it difficult to develop other skills? What are the implications for teaching and speech therapy? Finally, since sensory concerns are now considered a primary aspect of ASD (in the DSM-5), isn't it time we take a much closer look at sensory perception and sensory integration in the early years, and their consequences, so we can help these children adapt and progress? The time has come for us to listen carefully to the children and their stories, cherish their messages, and learn the life-changing lessons they have to offer.

9

Special Traits and Learning Styles

WONDERED WHY my students who had the echolalia trait also shared a similar style of learning. Might their common strengths and characteristics explain why they had followed a similar pathway to develop adaptive strategies? Was their "quirky" behaviour, as many professionals often describe echolalia, actually a neuroplastic detour or strategy that allowed them to circumvent their similar sensory and perceptual challenges? As we read between the lines of these "special traits," will we be able to discover what lies in the spaces we cannot see? Perhaps, but only if we are willing to look. That is the first step.

As Easy as ABC

I became aware that several of my students who shared the echolalia trait were also hyperlexic, and as children had delayed or regressive language development. Several of their families reported their children had compensated for their language challenges by learning to access speech through teaching themselves how to read. This is also similar to what the Gilman, Barnett, and Suskind families experienced. Benj Gilman relied on his precocious reading ability to develop his language skills and his love of poetry, Jake Barnett held fast to his alphabet letters when his verbal skills seemed to be disappearing, and Owen Suskind taught himself to read by repeatedly viewing the credits at the end of his favourite Disney movies.

All of these children seemed to share a similar style of learning and language development, relying on their visual learning skills, excellent auditory and visual memory capacity, and a propensity to "think in words." Temple Grandin's phrase "thinking across the spectrum" in its many forms and presentations directs us to consider the importance of different minds and learning styles for creating opportunities for successful outcomes. The various patterns of thinking are not mere quirks or bizarre behaviours that should be overlooked or dismissed out of hand, but instead suggest the need to further investigate the special traits of such unique, creative, and adaptive minds.

Oliver Sacks (1995, xvii) highlights this view and quotes developmental psychologist I.S. Vygotsky, who focused on abilities rather than deficits and in so doing recognized the value of unique minds: "A handicapped child represents a qualitatively different, unique type of development ... If a blind or deaf child achieves the same level of development as a normal child, then the child with a defect achieves in another way, by another course, by other means; and, for the pedagogue, it is particularly important to know the uniqueness of the course along which he must lead the child. This uniqueness transforms the minus of the handicap into the plus of compensation."

The children I've described all seem to have followed a similar developmental path. First, they demonstrate a precocious interest in the letters of the alphabet. Then they quickly move on to written words. A fascination with movies, cartoons, TV shows, books, poetry, or computer games soon follows. So is it all that surprising that these children, who taught themselves how to speak by teaching themselves to read, would now continue to "think in words" and rely on movies, books, and the characters within them as models for further language development? Letters, words, then phrases and even entire scripts are all effortlessly committed to memory and incorporated into the children's personal databases, tucked safely away in the recesses of their minds. Conversational exchanges or phrases can now serve as models to be studied, observed, and reviewed, over and over again, with freeze-frame accuracy. Dialogue can be internalized and then accessed and retrieved as needed as the children attempt to express their needs and develop conversational skills. These students all have strong auditory memories, as displayed by their ability to replicate with perfect, word-for-word accuracy, along with an uncanny ability to imitate voices and accents. This stands in stark contrast to their otherwise flat monotonic speech pattern, which they use during more prosaic exchanges. By watching favourite movies or shows over and over again, they begin to incorporate a large repertoire of conversational exchanges that can be called up and inserted into conversations when an appropriate situation presents itself.

When travelling in foreign countries, many people rely on phrasebooks to help them communicate if they are unfamiliar with the language. For individuals with ASD who struggle to communicate, scripts may serve a similar purpose, as they search for the right "phrase" from within their personal database of memorized dialogue.

I believe this extraordinary ability, contrary to common misconceptions, is actually driven by a strong need to communicate: even when faced with great sensory challenges, they persevere. Not in the obsessional sense, as reflected in the term *perseveration*, which is often associated with echolalia, but in the determined and effortful sense, when one carries on in the face of great obstacles. In fact, it demonstrates their strong desire to connect—but on their terms, using their strengths and abilities, and developing a different neural pathway that allows them to navigate their way toward rather than away from us. An impressive feat, and extremely resourceful!

"Thinking in scripts" may be the unique way in which some children adapt in order to acquire the language skills they need to understand human interactions, understanding that otherwise eludes them during the fast-paced exchanges of daily life. It also provides models that might explain human behaviour and provide important lessons about life. Isn't that one of the reasons we turn to literature, poetry, art, and drama—to find answers that might explain the mysteries of the human condition?

Often, when a situation in class reminded my students of a scene from a movie or TV show, they just couldn't resist expressing the connection. They were quite good at it, and I was often reminded of the late Robin Williams, a comic genius and brilliant improvisational comedian who could call up different characters, voices, dialogue from movies at just the right moment in order to brilliantly capture the essence of a person or event.

This ability is not much different from the ability—which we are usually impressed by—to commit parts of the Bible or Shakespeare to memory and then effortlessly and eruditely match them to the appropriate situation. Like Marc's "And me without my camera." (I'm still blushing…)

Special Abilities Come to Life in the Classroom

Unfortunately, the tendency for schools to remain focused on discrete behaviours, rather than on an understanding of learning profiles and patterns of thinking, still influences the way individual education plans (IEPs) are being developed today. While it is true that, as the saying goes, "if you know one child with autism, then you know one child with autism," it also holds true that as we learn more about different kinds of minds, as described by Temple Grandin and other researchers, we can also appreciate common characteristics and shared learning profiles that point to similar patterns of thinking and processing information.

Educators discovered the effectiveness of developing learning profiles when teaching students with learning disabilities, and I have found this approach to be equally effective when teaching students with ASD. When learning profiles are paired with compatible teaching approaches, success soon follows. In her book *Helping Children with Autism Learn: Treatment Approaches for Parents and Professionals*, Bryna Siegel ([2003] 2007) showed the importance of "finding the right method for your child's learning style" when considering the child's constellation of characteristics and abilities. This understanding also serves to enhance many of the effective evidenced-based programs in place today. Once we look beyond the behaviours of the "acting self" and begin to consider the educational needs of the "thinking self," opportunities for learning are soon revealed. Differentiated instruction recognizes the value of this understanding for everyone, "with no one left behind."

BRYNA SIEGEL

LORNA WING believed that to "acquire a depth of knowledge" about autism it is important "to work closely with children over many years, observing and interacting with them and listening with great attention to the parents' descriptions of their children's development from infancy. This cannot be done sitting comfortably on the other side of a desk in a consulting room. You have to be part of the action to see it for yourself." These words appear in Wing's foreword to *The World of the Autistic Child: Understanding and Treating Autistic Spectrum Disorders* by Bryna Siegel (1996). Wing and Siegel both recognized the value of learning from the children themselves, which is where true understanding and hope can be found.

In her seminal book *Helping Children with Autism Learn: Treatment Approaches for Parents and Professionals—A Guide to Autistic Learning Disabilites and Finding the Right Method for Your Child's Learning Style*, Siegel highlights the neurological nature of autism, linking it to the successful learning disabilities model of addressing strengths and weaknesses throughout the lifetime of individuals on the spectrum:

> The conceptualization of learning weaknesses and strengths is core to the whole field of learning disabilities and to compensatory educational approaches. For this reason, I've come to see autism as a learning disability syndrome, with each symptom connoting a related cluster of learning weaknesses or an area of "autism—specific" learning disability... Using autistic learning disabilities as the organizing construct, it is possible to reconceptualize treatment for autism... Reconceptualizing autism as a

learning disability syndrome is intended to help break disciplinary barriers. ([2003] 2007, 4–5)

This important book garnered the support of Temple Grandin as well as that of one of the leaders in the field of early intervention, Sally Rogers, a professor of psychiatry and behavioural sciences at the University of California Davis Medical Center's M.I.N.D. Institute. Together with her colleague Geraldine Dawson, Rogers developed the Early Start Denver Model, recognized internationally as a highly effective and practical program. Rogers (2015), like Siegel, recognizes that children with ASD are "magnificent learners," and explains that that "capitalizing on their learning strengths" will serve their interests and needs from the earliest interventions, well into their school years and throughout the rest of their lives.

Gary Mesibov, who endorsed Siegel's work in her book, *Getting the Best for Your Child with Autism: An Expert's Guide to Treatment*, supports her understanding of learning styles, which is similar to the TEACCH approach to learning.

Although Bryna Siegel has retired from the University of California, San Francisco, and its Autism Clinic (Langley Porter Psychiatric Institute), she remains very active as the founder and executive director of the Autism Center of California.

AUTISM SPEAKS CANADA Rogers 2015; Siegel 1996, 2003, 2008

Fred: My Personal GPS

I came to rely on many of my students' special talents, particularly on school outings. Many were fascinated by maps, easily committing them to memory after just one viewing, and they knew subway and travel routes by heart. I relied on them for help with preparations for school trips, as they planned the best route or suggested points of interest along the way. No need for Google Maps when my students were around! We always prepared a Plan B, as part of my strategy to help them develop more flexibility in the world of road closures and of delays and breakdowns of "trains, planes, and automobiles." We actually made a game of planning alternate routes and they really enjoyed it. When planned routes didn't work out, I would quickly ask the class, "What do we do?" In unison, they would reply, with great enthusiasm, "Plan B!" What had been a cause for anxiety and an unmanageable problem in the past had now become a manageable challenge.

The students were also helpful with roll call on school trips. Several of my students had an uncanny ability to keep track of everyone's whereabouts. I remember one trip in particular, when we were boarding the bus to return to school and a rather quiet student named Fred began shouting the name of a support staff member. We hadn't noticed that this staff member was missing, and thanks to Fred, we delayed our departure. Nobody left behind—well, not that day. On future trips, I always checked in with Fred, and he was proud of his new role as the assistant bus monitor.

Fred also had a keen interest in the public transit system and eventually was hired as a courier for Good Foot Delivery (goodfootdelivery.com), which is dedicated to employing adults like Fred who display an excellent knowledge of the transit system, equal to the famous black-cab drivers of

London. At last report, he was thrilled with his job and meeting other employees with similar interests.

Many other students demonstrated great facility with computers and intuitively navigated their way when interested in a particular topic. *They* frequently helped *me* figure out new applications, rather than the other way around; they just seemed to know how these things worked. I wondered if their ease with computers was a result of their particular cognitive processing style, which might be in sync with the logic and thinking patterns of computer designers and programmers. Clearly, my brain did not align with this way of thinking, and I would gratefully rely on my students instead of resorting to online tutorials or a call to the help desk.

Our class also enjoyed puzzles and we always had a communal puzzle on the go. When students felt they needed a break, they could choose to take time out and work on the puzzle. Cindy won the respect of the other students when they saw her use her special talent—completing a puzzle with the picture side facing down, relying only on the shapes of the pieces. I actually think she found the picture to be a bit of a distraction. And no one in our class had a problem solving the parking-lot puzzle. Give it a try yourself.

Parking Lot Puzzle

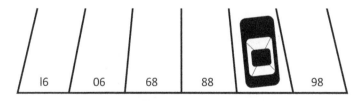

What is the number of the parking spot where the car is parked?

The correct answer to the puzzle is 87. My teaching colleagues and other "typical" professionals had difficulty solving this problem. Even when I gave them the correct answer, many still couldn't "see" it. But for my students, no problem. (I too got the correct answer, probably as a result of the positive influence from the many unique minds I've taught over the years.)

If you're still struggling, here is a hint: go back and look at the parking lot from the driver's perspective, and then look at the numbers from the driver's seat. You see, the answer relies on changing your point of view—taking the perspective of the driver of the car as well as noticing the nature of the numbers, which have the common characteristic of being read either from top to bottom or the reverse. Typical people tend to immediately rely on the logic of number sequencing, and use only that strategy, seeing the numbers from their own perspective, but that won't work. My students, on the other hand, easily and automatically viewed this problem from the driver's point of view, and it is precisely this ability to consider the problem from another person's viewpoint that allows you to figure it out. By using their "theory of mind," many of my students effortlessly solved the puzzle. Typical people, on the other hand, still struggled.

Words Come to Life in the Classroom

Suit the action to the word, the word to the action.

HAMLET *Act III, scene ii*

It has been observed that the pronoun *I* is not often used by children with ASD, who have a greater tendency to use their given name or the third-person pronoun (he/she). I believe their overreliance on observing other people, or characters from books or movies, is in large part responsible for reinforcing their confusion about the correct usage of pronouns; it's not an indication of loss of self, as many professionals in the field believe, but rather just another example of repeating what they hear. The tendency to model their behaviour and speech on those of others may result in their repeating exactly what they hear others say or repeating how others refer to them. When using other people as models and copying what they hear (echolalia), they can lose the personal pronouns like *I*.

Similarly, I noticed that my students often referred to their parents by their given names, since only the children in a family use *mom* or *dad*. An older child or an only child with ASD might tend to use what they hear used by others. Calling their parents by their given names, as many of my students did, is not an indication of detachment but rather just another example of their strong reliance on modelling their language on others and replicating what they hear.

I remember an occasion when our entire class went to visit a business office after a parent had invited us as part of a district-wide program called "Take Your Kid to Work." During our visit, I noticed that the parent's son, my student, stopped calling his father by his first name, as he usually did, but instead adopted the same name used by his father's employees— Mr. Smith.

Again, if we view this misuse of pronouns in psycholinguistic terms rather than from a purely behavioural perspective, effective strategies can be designed to address this problem. I realized that I needed to encourage my students to become their *own* role models. Their tendency to rely on other students or favourite characters to help them figure out what to do or say, while effective to a point, needed to transition toward creating a more personal visual representation of themselves carrying out various tasks in their mind's eye.

They would also need to be taught how to develop a more conventional speaking style when required, while still respecting their passion for "scripting." They needed to discover their own voice.

Personal stories can capitalize on the students' ability to model and from there develop their expressive language skills. But this time they can rely on themselves as the perfect model. I encouraged my students to compose personal stories as a way to improve both their expressive language skills and their social skills and ability to connect with their classmates. They created autobiographical booklets or storyboards with photos of themselves performing various tasks (using computer photo applications or simply pasting printed photos on cardboard or paper) and captions and dialogue they composed. The results were extremely positive. They could now play themselves in their own stories, becoming less reliant on others to "speak" for them; they could become their own role models instead of relying solely on characters from books and movies. In this way they could practice, rehearse, and internalize their own dialogue, which they could use later. It really is not much different from what's done in an English as a Second (or Learned) Language class; I also have experience with ESL teaching and found the same techniques suitable when working with my students with ASD.

Lights, Camera, Action: If in Doubt, Act It Out

Videotaping can also provide a way to help students use favourite characters not just as models to be copied but also as teachers who might help them discover their own voice and pathway toward more traditional dialogue. And the earlier such strategies are implemented, the greater the chances for success. I remember one father telling me that he reminded his son to "act as himself," and, to the father's delight, his son began using his own voice. Although the student continued to use memorized dialogue from movies when feeling anxious, it was a start.

Many of my students were natural performers and enjoyed acting out roles from favourite stories. I tried to encourage this natural ability yet at the same time limit and redirect it by presenting drama as the right context for it. In this way, they could begin to use their talents in a more appropriate time and place. The students also created puppet shows, with puppets of their own making, dramatizing many of the stories we read in class. For the students who spoke infrequently or were just learning to read, these performances helped them participate and access these stories in a different way. The students who read fluently sometimes acted as dialogue coaches and prompters, a role they enjoyed.

Whether the students had advanced reading skills or had never been taught to read beyond the very basic level, *all* responded well to the enriched individualized reading programs I developed for them and soon were borrowing books from the local library for the first time. Literacy for all was our credo. For Lauren, a student who preferred to spend much of her time alone until she was taught how to read, books changed everything; she quickly developed a love for all things Harry Potter and started a fan club at school, making many new friends in the process.

Paula Kluth and Kelly Chandler-Olcott (2008) refer to the provision of enriched literary experiences for all students using a variety of learning modalities as "multiple literacies." Sybil Elgar included the arts as an important feature of the Ealing School, and her students responded well as they began to explore and express their creative abilities. Drama, poetry, art, and music should be included as an important and necessary part of every student's school program. Art for art's sake—and for the sake of the children.

Carol Gray's Social Stories® is a social learning tool that helps children develop the social skills needed for everyday life.

carolgraysocialstories.com

An additional, and excellent, classroom resource is *The Hidden Curriculum: Practical Solutions for Understanding Unstated Rules in Social Situations* by Brenda Smith Myles, Melissa Trautman, and Ronda Schelvan.

Many of my students also displayed a keen interest in graphic novels and manga (a style of Japanese graphic novel), well-established literary genres that are extremely popular among high school students and particularly appealing to students with ASD, offering the same benefits as movies or TV shows, but somehow more up-close and personal. Today, graphic novels are part of the standard high school English curriculum; extensive collections are available at most school and public libraries. I frequently observed my students with their noses buried in their books, as if to get as close to the action as possible. They loved the graphics but were also attracted to the dialogue. Words and actions presented together seemed to deepen their understanding and enjoyment. No voice but their own brought these characters to life as they read these exciting and dynamic stories. They could read at their own pace, frame by frame, as they discovered their own comfort level with the material, flipping back and forth between the pages, lingering a little longer at a favourite scene. Like the letters of the alphabet, beloved characters could be studied and read over and over again, providing another way of understanding our complex world.

Many graphic novels use sophisticated dialogue and offer an opportunity to develop students' language skills. My students also enjoyed reading graphic novels aloud in groups, which offered a wonderful way to share common interests, socialize, and continue to appreciate the art of the novel. I soon began to notice a marked improvement in their language skills, and they looked forward to participating in our classroom book group discussions. Many of my students also enjoyed creating their own graphic stories, using digital software such as Comic Life, Bit Strips, and Pixton. (New and improved software is continually being developed. A recent recommendation was Scratch, which you can find at scratch.mit.edu.) Of course, the old-fashioned hand-drawing method was another wonderful option, and was preferred by some students. Claymation or stop-motion animation videos were popular, too, and they are easy and fun to create. I also encouraged my students to create stories they felt would help them prepare for a social event, a co-op placement, or even the much-anticipated graduation ceremony.

Howcast has an excellent video series on how to produce a claymation movie.

howcast.com/?s=claymation

Excellent guides to Lego storytelling include *Lego: Make Your Own Movie*, produced by KLUTZ; *Using Lego Therapy with Autistic Pupils*, by Claire Brodie and Vicky Mather; and *Lego-Based Therapy* by Daniel B. LeGoff, Gina Gómez de la Cuest, G.W. Krauss, and Simon Baron-Cohen.

My students' interest in stories is the same as my own. Books and movies capture life's lessons through the stories they tell. From an early age we all turn to stories to help us figure out the "human condition." So why should it be any different for children on the spectrum? Books and movies can be studied, replayed, and reread, helping guide children through the never-ending story of their lives. As Priscilla Gilman (2013) said in her *New York Times* article "Early Reader," "Characters from books helped Benj both understand and invent himself." When these cherished characters come to life in the classroom, and in the lives of families and communities, we all become part of the evolving story. So we should tread carefully before we dismiss as inconsequential and meaningless what is most valuable and precious, as we continue to read between the lines and discover the real story within. I was taught from a young age not to "judge a book by its cover," but instead to look deep within its pages. You never know what you might find.

As I've described, reading poetry was a popular activity in our class. We loved reading poems by Shel Silverstein, Dennis Lee, Robert Service, Ernest Thayer ("Casey at the Bat"), Lieutenant Colonel John McCrae ("In Flanders Fields"), and others. The rhythmic beat of poetry reinforced the spoken word, which now fell into a predictable pattern of rhythm and rhyme. This seemed to appeal to my students' attraction to patterns and the predictability within their designs, something that the prosaic conversations of daily life could not offer. Many of these poems are presented alongside wonderful drawings by famous artists, adding another dimension to their appeal, matching the sounds, rhythm, and meaning with the students' visual sensibilities. As we read these poems together in class, I noticed an immediate connection with this rhythmic presentation of language, as opposed to the simpler workbook stories (basal readers) the students were used to from the past, in which language was simplified and reduced to the most basic elements, stripped of its beauty and wonder, becoming stilted, lacklustre, unnatural, and, frankly, quite boring. Students need well-written stories that capture the imagination, the heart, the art of expression, and the rhythm of life. I encouraged students to make faces to match the feelings expressed in their favourite stories and poems and to make a game of it in the style of Simon Says. We also practiced making these faces in a mirror to help the students internalize the feelings with their own faces. We all found this to be rather hilarious and had a good laugh while making funny faces. They loved looking in the mirror and could begin to match the emotion with how it looked and felt within themselves. It was as though they were discovering a different part of themselves—as if meeting themselves for the first time.

Again, by becoming more aware of themselves as models and less reliant on others, they could begin to replace their stored pictures of others with images of themselves—images they could both see and feel as they began to develop a clearer image of themselves and become, in fact, more self-focused in order to become more self-reliant. Such is the paradoxical nature of ASD.

We also explored rap poetry and spoken word. I invited rap artists to perform in class as another way to bring words to life, and all of the students joined in, singing, clapping, drumming, and dancing. Everyone wanted to be a "star."

Poetry's gift was a part of Benj Gilman's life. Priscilla Gilman (2013, 39) encouraged her son and, by fourth grade, "Benj wrote several haunting haikus with images of ice and birch trees, cadences and rhythms straight out of the Frost poems he'd so loved as a child." Many of my students also wrote their own poems; acrostic poems were a particular favourite, along with other structured poetic forms.

In 1999, Sir Quentin Blake was appointed the first children's laureate in the UK. He encouraged children to discover the wonder of books, "both in their words and in their pictures" (2015, 1). Sir Quentin was asked by the National

Gallery to curate an art exhibition, which he called *Tell Me a Picture*. A picture is indeed worth a thousand words, and Sir Quentin encouraged children to write their comments on the gallery walls and "dialogue" with the famous works of art. (Fortunately, we too can participate in this "adventure in looking at art" with *Tell Me a Picture* in book form—a worthy addition to any school library.)

My students were particularly fond of Sir Quentin's collaborative work as an illustrator with Roald Dahl. *Matilda* was a class favourite, along with *The BFG*.

Reading between the Lines

The real challenge faced by many people on the spectrum lies not in words themselves but rather in what is not said, or what is meant or conveyed when we "read between the lines" of human exchanges. How do you decipher that "hidden code"—that which cannot be seen but nevertheless conveys another level of meaning? How do you interpret and understand beyond the literal?

In a famous scene from the movie *Annie Hall,* subtitles appear along with the dialogue to convey that what we say and what we mean are not necessarily one and the same. Standing on a balcony, Alvy and Annie are discussing photography, but if you believe that is the only thing they are talking about, then you have failed to pick up on the true meaning behind their words: Alvy is not really interested in photography, but he *is* interested in Annie. Similarly, Annie's words do not convey what she is really thinking. This scene cleverly pokes fun at us and the hidden meanings behind our words when we don't always say what we mean.

You can watch the balcony scene from *Annie Hall* on YouTube. A script of both the dialogue and subtitles is also available at AMC's Filmsite catalogue.

youtube.com/watch?
v=zMozdI8mhZ
filmsite.org/anni3.html

People on the spectrum tend to display a more honest approach when they communicate, for they say exactly what they mean, without pretense or guile. How refreshing to return to my classroom after attending yet another staff meeting where new special education labels and acronyms were assigned to old concepts as if being discovered for the first time. The special educational wheel invented anew, as we feigned enthusiasm lest we offend or appear unenlightened.

The words and labels keep changing but the mindset remains the same. What will it take for real change to take place? The integrity of my students makes me question our strange ways of connecting with each other, and I wonder how much is lost by not saying what we mean. What is the true lesson to be learned here, and who is the teacher? Maybe if we met halfway along the spectrum, each of us changing just a little, we might understand each other a little better. It's worth a try.

10

Rethinking
Eye Contact

AT THE AGE of sixteen, Kenny still rarely made eye contact. He was a kind, soft-spoken, and considerate student whose verbal exchanges were purposeful, to the point, and delivered in a rather monotone style. He was usually very quiet, except when singing in the community choir, which he still adores—his mellifluous tenor voice was suddenly awakened, transforming his entire being as he discovered a beautiful way to find harmony and connection with the world around him. His singing released emotions buried deep within his heart, now openly revealed with a sense of honesty and vulnerability. A more meaningful connection I cannot imagine.

He had learned to make eye contact when greeting people, but it was just that—contact rather than connection. Nevertheless, his warm and kind nature provided him with a more meaningful way of finding a connection with others, making him a very popular student, well-liked by all. Kenny has sensory sensitivities, and noisy environments can be upsetting, so he would often cover his ears to lessen the impact. He has perfect pitch and enjoyed listening to operas using his headphones. Kenny was also hyperlexic—that is, he taught himself how to read at a very early age. While he was slow to speak, his reading and speaking abilities appeared suddenly and simultaneously at around age three, as if the written word had been the key he needed to unlock and access the previously elusive world of speech through a different neural pathway, a "road less travelled," taken perhaps to bypass the confusing sensory world of sight, sound, and dynamic conversational exchanges.

Singing has allowed Kenny to find his true voice and to establish more meaningful connections that extend well beyond our welcoming eyes to a place deep within our hearts.

Hearing Lips

Even in adolescence, many of my students still demonstrated a level of disinterest with respect to eye contact. The issue was continually being addressed, yet it remained unresolved. And while they had learned to look at us when required, I noticed it wasn't something they had warmed to. But they had learned to manage and make eye contact when necessary for social reasons, for a co-op placement, or if requested. Other times they might initiate eye contact if they needed your immediate attention. Of course, these are important reasons to be able to make eye contact, but did they feel it helped their own understanding during conversations? I think not. Nevertheless, they were good sports about it and went along with it to please us as they tried to fit in.

So we have to ask: Does eye contact improve language acquisition skills, speech perception, comprehension, and communication skills for children with ASD in the same way it does for typical children? Or might it actually interfere with language acquisition and comprehension at certain stages of development? Perhaps there is a delicate balance to be found, where we can integrate the individual perceptual, sensory, and neurological challenges faced by children with ASD while helping them understand facial information and body language as they learn to integrate all the moving parts of conversational exchanges. And how do we find the fine balance necessary to integrate all of these diverse skills? I believe these are very important questions that we must ask as part of any therapy or educational program.

What You See Is Not Always What You Get

My adolescent students' ongoing lack of eye contact led me to believe that there are important neurodevelopmental and sensory issues at play that may result in the "symptom" of what appears to be eye avoidance (Moriuchi, Klin, and Jones 2017). My neuroscientific curiosity, along with my training in psycholinguistics and learning disabilities, made me want to investigate what was behind this lack of or need for eye contact. The research I discovered was fascinating.

Lack of eye contact is often cited as one of the main "behaviours" indicative of ASD. Yet it is actually the *absence* of a behaviour—that is, something a child is *not* doing—that arouses so much concern. Many people find the lack of eye contact disconcerting, and often believe (or hope) that correcting it early might ameliorate future difficulties related to personal connections and relationships, communication, and intellectual development. We therefore need to learn as much as possible about the nature of "eye gaze," in order to determine when and how to best address what lies behind this aspect of autism.

Lack of eye contact often appears during the early stages in a child's development, as parents are establishing close bonds of love and connection with their child. They soon start to notice the child seeming to evade their gaze or not responding to their name. Parents begin to feel cut off and disconnected from their child, leaving them unsure of where to turn or how to establish a close and meaningful connection. The feelings of loss, alienation, and disconnection can be devastating and the impact on families profound. The "sense" of isolation observed in the child is also deeply felt by every member of the family. And there is that underlying hope that, if eye contact returns, so might the close connection to their child.[1]

But if we find another way of considering "diminished eye looking" (Jones and Klin 2013), we might reach a different understanding and lessen that sense of loss and feeling of hopelessness. What if we consider the child's change in eye gaze as a response to their sensory environment and perceptual needs? By merely observing the "acting self" without the benefit of comprehending the underlying sensory and perceptual causes that contribute to the development of the symptom, we not only limit our understanding but may also miss out on the opportunity to devise helpful strategies that can address the causes and real language issues revealed by this symptom, rather than simply treating the symptom as a behaviour to be corrected in and of itself.

In other words, by "working with autism" with an appreciation for the sensory and perceptual challenges the child is experiencing, we might gain a deeper understanding of the neurodevelopmental and sensory issues that contribute to the development of the symptom of diminished eye looking. If we see past the outward expression of ASD, we just might discover another way of connecting with the inner life of the child as we continue our efforts to establish a meaningful and caring relationship. For therein lies real hope for realizing a child's full potential.

Neurotypicals, even many professionals, tend to view lack of eye contact as primarily a socially problematic behaviour, which they believe impedes the development of language, intellectual development, and effective communication. But does it? Or might it be the other way around, with sensory and language problems impeding the development of the ability to manage additional sensory information from facial expressions, eye contact, and body language, which then impacts social development (as already noted by Wing, Schopler, and Rutter)?[2]

First, let's define what we mean by communication skills. We have non-verbal social communication skills, such as facial expressions and body language, as well as verbal language skills, such as speech perception, language acquisition, and sensory perception/processing, all of which work together during our interactions with people. What role does eye contact play in each of these areas, for both typical children and children with ASD, and how might this influence therapy treatments and teaching methods? For children with ASD and sensory challenges, it is important to not confuse the social aspect of communication with the language processing aspect. Children with ASD may not follow the same sequence of integrative steps and stages in relation to speech perception and language development as typical children do. Therefore, we need to understand more about language acquisition and speech perception, along with the particular neurological and sensory implications associated with the development of these skills for individuals with ASD.

ASD is first and foremost a neurodevelopmental exceptionality, which suggests the possibility of an atypical path of perceptual and cognitive development, not unlike that encountered in those with learning disabilities. Developmental delays or differences may result, as more time and practice may be needed at various stages of development in order for these children to experience and integrate all the multisensory modalities of speech perception as one unified sensation (percept). A child may develop their own ways of compensating for their difficulties, and these strategies provide us with valuable insights as we try to figure out the child's strengths and weaknesses. Educators trained in this type of assessment learn to look beyond presenting behaviours for hidden strengths and abilities. Therapies and remedial techniques that recognize and understand these challenges will require a more nuanced bridging of atypical and typical skill development, along with an awareness of the diverse and varied sensory challenges experienced by each child.

In *Teaching Autistic Children*, Wing and Elgar describe the children's behaviour as being closely connected to their sensory and perceptual experiences:

> The children behave as if they cannot make sense of the information which comes to them through their senses, especially those of hearing and vision. Their eyes and ears are usually normal. The trouble comes when the information reaches the brain. It seems as if the impression from the outside world cannot be made into a clear and coherent picture, but remain a confused and frightening jumble of fleeting impressions. Watching a young autistic child and the way he reacts suggests that sometimes visual impressions and sounds do not get through to him at all, sometimes he is extremely oversensitive and finds light and sound painful and distressing, and sometimes he is

completely fascinated by simple sense impressions such as a flickering light or the noise of a friction drive toy. The children seem to be unable to distinguish the things which are important from those which are trivial. This seems to be closely connected with the difficulty they have in developing an understanding of symbols and abstract ideas, and hence to the poverty of their language development... It could be argued that the perceptual problems are primary, but it is equally if not more likely that the lack of ability to use symbols affects the way the children respond to their environment from early life, and that this is the underlying difficulty. The problem will be solved only by careful observation and research, including work with very young autistic children, comparing their development with that of normal babies. (1969, 5)

Perhaps these behaviours can now be seen more as strategies, different "forks in the road" to be followed, which children on the spectrum may develop as a consequence of trying to manage their sensory difficulties while they struggle to process all of the moving parts of human discourse embedded in a sensory environment. But clearly, the desire and wish to understand what is being said is evident if we consider the lack of eye contact through the "eyes" of "the thinking self." Perception is in the eye of the beholder.

My years of teaching convinced me that sensory issues lie at the heart of ASD, with other challenges emerging as a consequence of this aspect of the child's neurological make-up. It then becomes a chicken-and-egg dynamic, making it difficult to see the chain of events beyond that which is expressed by the "acting self." I was also curious about the way my students tried to adapt in light of their receptive language challenges, and instead employed different strategies, more in line with their perceptual strengths but perhaps appearing as odd or strange to typical people.

I've also observed which behaviours or strategies individuals on the spectrum develop as a result or consequence of their sensory/perceptual challenges. Once we identify their dominant processing modality, along with the adaptive strategies they have developed on their own, we may be in a better position to design a remedial plan matched to their particular needs and style of learning.

In *The Autistic Brain* (2013), Temple Grandin wrote about the different types of learning styles, and this important information suggests that we need to take a closer look at what is going on. Sybil Elgar was also aware of the diverse thinking patterns of her students when she described her innovative, effective, and progressive teaching methods as far back as 1969:

> [T]eachers know... some children think in predominately visual terms while others form mental images mainly in words... Fortunately many techniques are available which can be applied once the syndrome is recognized and a "learning block" diagnosed. The supplementary use of touch and movement and auditory aids for children with visual problems... are all being used in ordinary schools. These methods cannot, of course, be taken over uncritically for autistic children... one does not need to begin again.

Elgar then explained the consequential nature of behaviours:

> [N]o two autistic children are alike... there is still no substitute for individual trial and error in discovering the best way forward... The child has difficulty in understanding

what is said and he has difficulty in expressing what he wants to say... He is not deliberately disobedient and, when he does become able to grasp the meaning of the words, controlling his behaviour becomes much simpler... These are "secondary" disabilities although to the parent and to the inexperienced teacher, they are the most obvious features of the child's behaviour.

Elgar explains that behaviour problems can disappear as the children mature and are helped to understand the world around them:

[T]he development of odd routines or rituals... should be regarded as a healthy attempt to make sense out of a confusion of sensory experience, utilizing whatever skills and knowledge the child has been able to acquire... but, with maturation, with firm handling and... positive teaching methods... simple behaviour can be replaced by more complicated and constructive activity... other common behavioural problems, such as destructiveness or screaming or self-injury or withdrawal, should not be regarded as insuperable obstacles to teaching. (J. Wing [1966] 1969, 206-11)

So if we redirect our attention and look a little differently at what is going on, considering a lack of eye contact, as Elgar suggests, "as a healthy attempt to make sense out of a confusion of sensory experience, utilizing whatever skills and knowledge the child has been able to acquire," we then might ask: Is the child simply eye avoidant, or are they doing something else, something they may need to do as a way of compensating for a deficit or sensory challenge?

I tried to listen to what my students were trying to communicate, as they patiently waited for me to figure it out. In my experience, I've never met a student who did not want to communicate, and I believe a genuine drive to express needs and wishes is ever-present. Having difficulty communicating is not the same as not wanting to communicate.

Seeing Things Differently

Many people with ASD have said that eye contact can in fact interfere with communication rather than improve it; if it were helpful, once introduced to the skill, they would use it, yet many still resist.

This can be seen in many of the autobiographies written by people on the spectrum. For example, in *The Reason I Jump: The Inner Voice of a Thirteen-Year-Old Boy with Autism*, Naoki Higashida's response to the question "Why don't you make eye contact when you're talking?" is both poignant and informative:

> True, we don't look at people's eyes very much. "Look whoever you're talking with properly in the eye," I've been told, again and again and again, but I still can't do it. To me making eye contact with someone I'm talking to feels a bit creepy, so I tend to avoid it.
>
> Then where exactly am I looking? You might well suppose that we're just looking down, or at the general background. But you'd be wrong. What we're actually looking at is the other person's voice. Voices may not be visible things, but we're trying to listen to the other person with all of our sense organs. When we're fully focused on working out what the heck it is you're saying, our sense of sight sort of zones out. If you can't make out what you're seeing, it's the same as not seeing anything at all.

What's bothered me for a long time is this idea people have that so long as we're keeping eye contact while they're talking to us, that alone means we're taking in every word. Ha! If only that was all it took, my disability would have been cured a long time ago. (2013, 25)

Higashida's words provide valuable insights, for he explains that eye contact may interfere with his struggle to integrate sight and sound in his effort to develop more effective communication skills.

In Higashida's case, and many others, if you look past current assumptions regarding eye contact and instead see it as a consequence of a unique way of "working out what the heck it is you're saying," you will discover a bright and articulate adolescent who, in spite of his challenges, comprehends and expresses himself quite well, and this should both allay our fears and concerns and arouse our curiosity to learn more about how he manages in spite of his deficits. But many neurotypicals, including many professionals and educators, still resist this view, continuing instead to see the lack of eye contact as a behavioural or social problem, which they then believe creates a barrier to intellectual development and effective communication. They can't seem to see past the "acting self" to accept the neurological viewpoint of the "thinking self" as described by Higashida and as I observed in my own students. So, who is right and who is wrong? Or is it just a question of perspective, of understanding and seeing and hearing, and perceiving things differently?

THE AUTISTIC RELATIONSHIP

THE CURIOUS thing about ASD and its impact on communication and social interactions is that it is a condition that involves other people. We are part of the "autistic relationship," for communication cannot exist in isolation. (Clinical psychologist Tony Attwood [2007, 55–56] has also described the relational dimension for ASD.) ASD is realized in our relationships, involving at least two people who may have very different methods and styles of communicating and may be out of sync with each other—the neurotypical person and the person with ASD, each resisting the other.

In keeping with my diagnostic and psycholinguistic training, I not only asked why my students preferred to look away from the eyes, with the standard answer being because eye contact makes them uncomfortable or because they have autism, but went further and asked: What are they doing instead, and why? And what does Higashida mean when he asks, "Then where exactly am I looking?"

Seeing Voices

So what does the research on speech perception and language processing actually tell us about the way typical people process language, and whether it's the same or different for individuals on the spectrum? I set about searching for more information about speech perception for both neurotypicals and individuals with ASD and discovered some fascinating research that both surprised and pleased me.

But first, it is important for us to understand typical child development with respect to language acquisition and speech perception to gain an even deeper appreciation of how the brain processes and perceives information. The research on speech perception can then also help us understand eye contact from a more neurodevelopmental perspective, thereby giving us a deeper appreciation for the way different minds make sense of our dynamic and noisy world. This helpful guideline was suggested by Lorna Wing (1972, 56): "[A] teacher is one member of the team which should be concerned about helping an autistic child ... She needs to have knowledge and experience of normal child development and of teaching normal children, so that she can recognise the stages in the progress of an autistic child, and not mistake immature behaviour for a pathological symptom."

Remember, "it is hard for a free fish to understand what is happening to a hooked one."

The McGurk Effect and
the Mystery of Speech Perception

What we're actually looking at is the other person's voice.

NAOKI HIGASHIDA

Today, many people, including many professionals in the field of ASD, still believe that typical speech perception is essentially an auditory process. This misconception continues to influence many current approaches to treatment and therapy for children with ASD, without considering the receptive language needs a child may be experiencing when trying to integrate sensory stimuli during the early years of language development.

Yet cognitive psychologist Harry McGurk proved otherwise in 1976, pointing to the important influence of the visual modality—that is, reading lips—on the way we all perceive and process language. Here, I revisit McGurk's groundbreaking work, along with the findings of current researchers who have examined the nature of eye gaze and its impact on both neurotypicals and individuals on the spectrum. This should prompt us to review the implications of this work in enhancing contemporary treatments and approaches within a more psycholinguistic and neurological framework.

The McGurk effect, or illusion, was first described by McGurk himself, along with his colleague, John MacDonald, in a letter they wrote to the journal *Nature* entitled, "Hearing Lips and Seeing Voices," in which they set out to solve the mystery of speech perception in typical development. Here is how they explained their findings, describing the previously unrecognized influence of vision and watching the mouth on speech perception:

> Most verbal communication occurs in contexts where the listener can see the speaker as well as hear him. However, speech perception is normally regarded as a purely auditory process. The study reported here demonstrates a previously unrecognised influence of vision upon speech perception. It stems from an observation that, on being shown a film of a young woman's talking head, in which repeated utterances of the syllable [ba] had been dubbed on to lip movements for [ga], normal adults reported hearing [da] ... When these subjects listened to the soundtrack from the film, without visual input, or when they watched untreated film, they reported the syllables accurately as repetitions of [ba] or [ga]. Subsequent replications confirm the reliability of these findings; they have important

implications for the understanding of speech perception. (1976, 746)

Note that the illusion of perceiving the sound [da] rather than either [ba] or [ga] demonstrates how the brain has found a way to reconcile the discrepancy between the modalities of vision and audition by perceiving a different sound from what was acutally uttered or mouthed, a sort of middle ground, a very diplomatic solution on the part of the brain. The McGurk effect teaches us much about how the brain processes sensory information, demonstrating that what you see or hear is not always what you get.

"Horizon: Is Seeing Believing?" on BBC2 lets you experience the McGurk effect for yourself, so you can better appreciate its implications. You can watch it on YouTube.

youtube.com/watch?v= G-IN8vWm3mo

During speech perception, what we hear or see is often a result of what the brain enables us to perceive, in spite of normal hearing and visual acuity, and is based on a greater collaboration of the different senses within the context of both verbal and non-verbal information in the interest of efficient or "good enough" comprehension. McGurk and MacDonald's finding captured the multisensory nature of speech perception as more of a team effort, often referred to as multisensory integration and perception. When discrepancies arise during normal daily conversations, as a result of noise, distractions, or fast-paced dialogue, where sight and sound may seem out of sync, we might unconsciously look at the mouth to help us figure out an unclear or misheard word— what I refer to as, "If in doubt, look at the mouth."

Illusions like the McGurk effect can teach us so much about the processing of sensory information within the brain, reminding us that what you see or hear is not always what you get. The McGurk effect clearly demonstrates that what we "hear" (perceive) is not always what was vocalized by the speaker but is rather a result of how the brain perceives and processes sight and sound.

McGurk and MacDonald's (1976, 747) experiment demonstrates that as the brain attempts to perceive this synchronized but conflicting representation of sight and sound as one unified sensation (percept) or experience, the result is often "a fused response ... where information from the two modalities is transformed into something new with an element not presented in either modality," resulting in what they refer to as "auditory-visual illusions."

By presenting mismatched pairings of sight (mouth) and sound (ear), the McGurk effect captures what can happen outside of natural conversational exchanges, when the brain is simply operating as a decoder without the benefit of meaning or influences from other cueing systems, such as syntax, semantics, tone, body language, or facial expressions, which might otherwise change what is perceived. McGurk was able to isolate sight and sound, thereby shining a light on the previously unknown influence of the visual modality (that is, watching the mouth) over the auditory (that is, hearing what is said).

The McGurk effect suggests that the brain has learned over time to rely on a frequently used neural pathway established by sight and sound during the typical stages in the development of efficient speech perception; that is, when we have difficulty hearing what is being said, our "back-up support" pathway ("if in doubt, look at the mouth") kicks in. Once learned, the neural pathways are formed and cannot easily be undone. By capturing this neuroplastic tendency or strategy in isolation, as purely a decoding exercise, McGurk was able to demonstrate the influence of vision as part of the well-established synchronized and multisensory neural pathway of speech perception, which is still ever-present even in its purest form, far removed from natural conversation. That is why, as McGurk and MacDonald (1976, 747) explained, "We ourselves have experienced these effects on many hundreds of trials; they do not habituate over time, despite objective knowledge of the illusion involved. By merely closing the eyes, a previously heard [da] becomes [ba] only to revert to [da] when the eyes are open again." This statement is somewhat ironic, because it in fact alerts us to an example of habituation, just not the one McGurk is referring to; for while McGurk thought an awareness of the illusion might undo the effect over time, the neural pathway ("if in doubt, look at the mouth") was already too well entrenched to be easily undone, and therefore did "not habituate over time, despite objective knowledge of the illusion involved." McGurk unwittingly captured neuroplasticity at its best, with no need for MRIs or brain scans. (No literature on the McGurk effect, as far as I know, has taken up these points as I have in this book.)

In their letter to *Nature*, McGurk and MacDonald did not offer a neuroplastic explanation for the effect, as the "fixed" and "hard-wired" view of brain structure was the more generally accepted view at the time. But they nevertheless captured the essence of a neuroplastic explanation in their observations, revealing the paradoxical nature of neuroplasticity: the brain is highly adaptable but also has a tendency to become entrenched when a pathway "habituates over time" as a necessary strategy. This is good news, for the brain's adaptability suggests that there may be optimum moments or opportunities that might allow for effective therapies or treatments for anyone, at any stage of life, when challenges arise as a result of developmental delays, sensory issues, or injury or illness.

McGurk's demonstration of the significant influence of the visual modality on speech perception for neurotypicals may suggest a more pronounced need for some individuals with ASD to focus on the mouth when they are struggling to integrate sight and sound. For other individuals, relying on their auditory skills by looking away may improve their receptive language skills, just as McGurk experienced: "By merely closing the eyes, a previously heard [da] becomes [ba] only to revert to [da] when the eyes are open again." If keeping our eyes closed ensures greater accuracy, what might that reveal about the way some children on the spectrum may choose to adapt when integrating sight and sound becomes too overwhelming? What does it tell us about the relationship between our senses and our brain?

Not everyone is affected by the McGurk effect. McGurk's research points to the emerging development of the effect as typical children age. The papers and articles listed below provide interesting investigations into the varied responses to the McGurk effect, particularly the research that examines the responses of children and adults with ASD and their implications for language development, learning, and sensory perception:

"Skilled Musicians Are Not Subject to the McGurk Effect," Alice Proverbio et al., 2016; available at nature.com/articles/srep30423

"Behavioral, Perceptual, and Neural Alterations in Sensory and Multisensory Function in Autism Spectrum Disorder," Sarah Baum et al., 2015; available at dx.doi.org/10.1016/j.pneurobio.2015.09.007

"Multisensory Temporal Integration in Autism Spectrum Disorders," Ryan Stevenson et al., *Journal of Neuroscience* 34, 2014

"Multisensory Speech Perception in Children with Autism Spectrum Disorders," Tiffany Woynaroski et al., *Journal of Autism and Developmental Disorders* 43, 2013

As I read McGurk and MacDonald's letter in *Nature*, I was reminded of the first pages of Temple Grandin's book *The*

Autistic Brain (2013, 3-4), when she describes her own struggle with language and speech perception in her early years: "Even though I was not deaf, I had difficulty hearing consonants, such as the c in cup. When grownups talked fast, I heard only vowels, so I thought they had their own special language. But by speaking slowly, the speech therapist helped me to hear the hard consonant sounds, and when I said cup with a c, she praised me—which is just what a behavioral therapist would do today." Grandin's comments uncannily and unwittingly captured exactly what McGurk realized might result when a child struggles to integrate sight and sound during speech perception, when words tend to move at a rather fast pace.

These important insights about the dynamic and multisensory nature of perceiving and processing sensory information have important implications for language acquisition in the early years. Working with a speech therapist—slowing down, and being taught the skills needed to integrate sight and sound—was beneficial for Grandin, who eventually spoke by the age of five.

With an appreciation for the multisensory nature of speech perception, a much stronger foundation can be established on which to build the skills required to integrate additional social and emotional information from the face, eyes, and body— step by incremental step. A better understanding of speech perception and its attending sensory challenges may further enhance many of the excellent programs already being used today.

Grandin's early struggles and McGurk's findings point to the importance of multimodal synchronicity during the developmental stages of speech perception and draw our attention to the problems and behaviours that may result when sight and sound are experienced too quickly to be fully integrated. For individuals on the spectrum, an overreliance on lip reading, rather than eye avoidance, may now be viewed as an adaptive skill used to integrate sight and sound during dynamic conversational exchanges.

Read My Lips

McGurk's findings also reminded me of the important work by Ami Klin, a leader in autism research and currently director of the Marcus Autism Center at Emory University School of Medicine. In 2002, Klin and his colleagues tracked the eye movements of individuals with ASD while they watched lively conversational exchanges taking place between the protagonists in the famous film adaptation of *Who's Afraid of Virginia Woolf*, by the playwright Edward Albee. The researchers not only confirmed the tendency of the ASD participants in the study to pay less attention to the protagonists' eyes, but also discovered that many of the participants actually preferred looking at the protagonists' mouths.

A photo from the study demonstrates this particular finding:

Visual focus of an autistic man and a normal comparison subject shown a film clip of a conversation. IMAGE © KLIN, AMI, WARREN JONES, ROBERT SHULTZ, FRED VOLKMAR, AND DONALD COHEN. (2002). "DEFINING AND QUANTIFYING THE SOCIAL PHENOTYPE IN AUTISM." *AM/PSYCHIATRY* 159 (JUNE): 6.

Most interesting of all, the researchers noted that "the more the participants focused on mouths, the more socially competent they were." Interestingly, this runs counter to what many professionals assume—that is, that more eye contact leads to improved social competence. Klin (Klin et al. 2002, 906) and his colleagues said, "This result raised the possibility that by focusing on mouths these individuals with autism might attain some understanding of social situations (perhaps because of greater, focused attention on speech), whereas attention to eyes may not lead to any additional social insights."

I believe these researchers' observations, taken together with McGurk's findings, not only move us even closer to considering what individuals with ASD are not doing, but also invite us to observe and consider the significance of what they *are* doing—that is, looking at the mouth or looking away from the face altogether in order to further reduce the experience of sensory overload.

This sounds similar to Naoki Higashida's experiences. Visual learners may tend to look at the mouth and auditory learners may choose to look away, and, in some cases, they may present a preferred ear with their head slightly tilted. Eye avoidance might then be viewed as the default position or consequence of the greater need to look at the mouth or turn away.

The McGurk experiment reveals the dynamic relationship that exists between sight and sound and, taken together with Klin and his colleagues' observations of the tendency to watch the speakers' mouths, raises some important questions about speech perception for individuals with ASD and the way the brain adapts when trying to integrate and process all the sensory information that occurs during dynamic conversational exchanges.

Language Development in the Early Years

For very young children in the early stages of language development, speech is initially perceived as a series of sounds and utterances, not unlike what is experienced with the McGurk effect. For children with sensory issues, language acquisition and speech perception can be an even greater challenge as they try to integrate all the sensations rapidly coming their way. I was curious about how the McGurk effect was experienced by typical children. McGurk and MacDonald's (1976, 747) findings highlighted its developmental aspects: "[W]here responses are dominated by a single modality, this tends to be the auditory for children and the visual for adults." This is quite significant, for it not only points to the emerging and dynamic nature of the effect, but also suggests opportunities to better understand and, if necessary, address any sensory issues or adaptive strategies that might compromise a child's language acquisition abilities during the developmental stages of speech perception.

McGurk's investigation of the developmental nature of the illusion as children age reminded me of a more recent study by Warren Jones and Ami Klin (2013), which indicated that eye looking "is not immediately diminished in infants later diagnosed with autism; instead, eye looking appears to begin at normative levels prior to decline."

When do we first notice a change as some children begin to look away from our welcoming eyes, while we continue to try to catch their gaze and maintain a close and meaningful connection?

"ATTENTION TO EYES IS PRESENT BUT IN DECLINE IN 2–6-MONTH-OLD INFANTS LATER DIAGNOSED WITH AUTISM"

IN THEIR study, Warren Jones and Ami Klin present some important findings:

> [I]nfants later diagnosed with autism spectrum disorders (ASDs) exhibit mean decline in eye fixation from 2 to 6 months of age, a pattern not observed in infants who do not develop ASD. These observations mark the earliest known indication of social disability in infancy, but also falsify a prior hypothesis: in the first months of life, this basic mechanism of social adaptive action—eye looking—is not immediately diminished in infants later diagnosed with ASD: instead, eye looking appears to begin at normative levels prior to decline. The timing of decline highlights a narrow developmental window and reveals the early derailment of processes that would otherwise have a key role in canalizing typical social development. Finally, the observation of this decline in eye fixation—rather than outright absence—offers a promising opportunity for early intervention that could build on the apparent preservation of mechanisms subserving reflexive initial orientation towards the eyes. (2013, 1)

How are we to understand what appears to be an emerging disconnection as the child begins to have less eye contact? What causes this change in "eye looking" and how might it correlate to a particular period in language acquisition and speech perception, which then impacts social abilities? Perhaps the child begins looking less to our eyes and more toward the mouth, or in other instances turns away from the face altogether, in order to focus on one stimulus (auditory) as a way to improve rather than impede speech perception, as the demands of processing language become more complex. The consequence of this adaptation may be diminished social skills, sacrificed in the process of "trying to remain fully focused on working out what the heck it is you're saying," as Higashida (2013, 25) reminds us. (Klin et al. [2002] noted that lip readers had better, though still problematic, social skills.)

With infants, we tend to model and present language to match their stage of development—first with simplified sounds and short syllables, pronounced slowly and clearly (e.g., "ma-ma"), then single words, then short sentences, continually adding to the complexity of what will be processed as children move through the various stages of speech perception and language acquisition. I wonder at which stage a child may begin to look away from the eyes, and what the implications are for appropriate intervention?

Jones and Klin's most recent work continues to explore many of the misconceptions regarding eye gaze. This is very exciting work, and I look forward to learning more from their ongoing research.

THE RESULTS of Moriuchi, Klin, and Jones' (2017) recent study, *Mechanisms of Diminished Attention to Eyes in Autism* "falsify the gaze aversion hypothesis; instead, at the time of initial diagnosis, diminished eye-looking in autism is consistent with passive insensitivity to the social signals in others' eyes."

The McGurk effect/illusion and the Jones and Klin research allow us to get a closer look at how the brain perceives and processes information. The term "speech perception" itself highlights the important role the brain plays in this sensory process, for this is where the real action takes place.

Do we all experience and "see" the world in exactly the same way? Don't we need to "hear" and "see" what is exact and true in order to have an accurate understanding of our world? Maybe not.

Perception Is in the Mind of the Beholder

The brain is locked in total darkness, of course, children, says the voice. It floats in a clear liquid made inside the skull, never in the light. And yet the world it constructs in the mind is full of light. It brims with color and movement. So how, children, does the brain which lives without a spark of light build for us a world full of light?

ANTHONY DOERR *All the Light We Cannot See*

So what *is* perception? It seems that what we end up seeing and hearing (i.e., perceiving) has more to do with the brain/mind and less to do with the eyes/ears. To understand perception and how we experience the world, we must look past the "acting self" and search for the answers within the "thinking self," for there is still so much to be uncovered. Unusual perceptions or illusions, far from being meaningless, tell us much about the inner workings of the mind, and that is where we just might find what is really going on.

Figure/Ground Dynamic:
Now You See It, Now You Don't

We can't possibly manage all of the information coming our way during our daily lives without feeling overwhelmed. We just need to see the "big picture" and focus on the details only when necessary. In this context the whole is greater than the parts as we go about our daily lives. But our perceptions and focus can change depending on the task at hand, and learning to efficiently manage the details (the figures) as well as the big picture (the figures in relation to the ground) can be both a strength and a weakness, depending on the context. This juggling of perception and focus is dynamic in nature but may present a challenge to some individuals on the spectrum. This skill is not unlike the depth-of-field function in an SLR camera, which can change the focus to suit the purpose or artistic sensibility of the user.

The invisible gorilla illusion described in the fascinating book co-authored in 2010 by Christopher Chabris and Daniel Simons, *The Invisible Gorilla and Other Ways Our Intuitions Deceive Us*, highlights the interesting influence of the figure/ground dynamic and the different ways individuals perceive the world.

Asked to count the basketballs being rapidly passed between players during a practice, many viewers fail to notice the person dressed in the gorilla suit who also appears on the court; their focus on counting the balls seems to make the "gorilla" invisible during this task.

Do such illusions help or impede our understanding of the world? Are they simply interesting parlour tricks or are they something more? Are perceptions exact representations of all that is before us, or, more likely, are they "good enough" representations of our environment, allowing us to accomplish tasks as we navigate our way through our dynamic, fast-paced world? Is "what we see" more accurately expressed as "what we *perceive*"—as we learn through experience which information is relevant and which can be ignored, filtering out what is extraneous and might otherwise interfere with our ability to handle all the information around us? This is in fact what the McGurk effect demonstrates: "good enough" efficiency trumps accuracy, and the end justifies the less accurate means. The dancing gorilla disappears or reappears depending on the task the brain wishes to accomplish. Perception is in the *mind* of the beholder.

You can experience the invisible gorilla illusion yourself on the website of Daniel Simons, head of the Visual Cognition Laboratory at the University of Illinois. His TEDx talk, "Seeing the World as It Isn't," is also worth a watch—you can find it on the same page.

dansimons.com/ videos.html

Our perceptions and what we perceive seem to be matched to the task we need to perform. They need to adapt when presented with different purposes, sometimes seeing the forest and sometimes just the trees; sometimes the basketballs and sometimes the gorilla. Too rigid a focus may result in misperceptions that could compromise our ability to adapt, for we need to move back and forth between figure and ground as the task demands.

Sometimes *too* accurate a focus, based on fine details, can take hold and interfere with the ability to take in the bigger picture. At the same time, an "eye for fine detail" and a more narrow focus can also be considered a strength and may lead to career opportunities. It is not either/or, but both/and.

So how do we develop the ability to move back and forth within this figure/ground dynamic? Do some individuals on the spectrum struggle when trying to shift their focus in figure/ground situations? How do we encourage the use of both skills without sacrificing special abilities in the process?

The experience of N.S., a young man with an extraordinary ability for seeing fine detail and detecting patterns, captures the challenge of recognizing this ability as a strength and as an opportunity to address the social costs that may accompany such abilities. To see his skill as simply quirky and odd, or as antisocial behaviour, would serve only to further isolate a very engaging individual. Thankfully, his strengths *were* recognized, resulting in a more positive social experience, as described in a story on the online news magazine *Forward*:

> A few years ago N.S., who has autism, thought the Israel Defense Forces wouldn't take him... N.S. ... spent his childhood in mainstream classroom settings, where he had focused on studying film and Arabic, but expected to miss out on being drafted—a mandatory rite of passage for most Israeli 18-year-olds.
>
> Now, more than a year into his army service, N.S. is a colonel who spends eight hours a day doing what few other soldiers can: using his exceptional attention to detail and intense focus to analyze visual data ahead of missions. Soldiers with autism can excel at this work because they are often adept at detecting patterns and maintaining focus for long periods of time.
>
> "It gave me the opportunity to go into the army in a significant position where I feel that I'm contributing," he said. (Sales 2015)

Recognizing his strengths also gave N.S. the chance to develop his weaker social skills alongside his strong attention to detail, in the company of others with common interests and goals, each enhancing the other.

While it is understandable that many children appear frustrated by their sensory and perceptual challenges, or find social situations to be challenging, we should view their frustration as more of a consequence of their challenges, rather than as simply a symptom of ASD or an unwillingness to socialize with others. The children have had to adjust to their sensory challenges on their own by developing adaptive and compensatory skills that may appear on the surface to be unusual "behaviours."

Having difficulty with communication and not wanting to communicate should not be viewed as one and the same. As yet, I have not met a student who did not display the need or desire to express themselves and be understood. Everyone has something to contribute; everyone belongs. N.S. was finally accepted for who he was and felt that he was contributing.

The Ames Distorted Room Illusion: What You See Is *Not* What You Get

Illusions like the McGurk effect and the invisible gorilla have much to teach us about the way the brain perceives or misperceives sensory information. This is not unlike what happens in the Ames Distorted Room Illusion, a sort of visual version of the McGurk effect. Temple Grandin (1986, 88) herself was fascinated by this illusion and was challenged by her teacher, Mr. Brooks, to solve the puzzle: "He explained that the Distorted Room is built in such a way that it tricks one's eye. When two people of the same height stand on each side of the room, one person looks twice as tall as the other. Mr. Brooks

Levitt Group Project

asked me, 'Can you make a room like this? I won't tell you how. I just want to see if you can figure it out.'" And she does.

Once Grandin understood the "trick," all became clear. We too must look within the "thinking self" to better understand sensory perception and from there develop a deeper appreciation for the relationship between the mind and the senses. Solving puzzles like the Ames Distorted Room Illusion helps us understand why individuals may misperceive sensory information, and moves us closer to addressing many of the mysteries of the brain and the implications for individuals on the spectrum.

Our brains are plastic and highly adaptable and that is a very good thing: it provides us with hope when faced with injury or illness and helps us appreciate the value of the road less travelled when we lose our way. The brain itself is essentially "blind and deaf," for its role is to interpret sensory stimuli regardless of how the information is transmitted. The brain doesn't really care how it gets the information.

For the brain, the ends justify the means. Exceptional and adaptive skills like what we see in the McGurk effect, pronounced lip reading, turning the head to present a preferred ear, hyperlexia, and other adaptations like echolocation (a strategy used by some individuals with vision impairments) are all excellent examples of the brain's ability to adapt to perceptual challenges.

The 2010 movie *Temple Grandin* includes a scene about the Ames Distorted Room Illusion. You can watch the clip on YouTube.

youtube.com/watch?v=chxCNESu3YU

FLASHES OF SOUND, OR "FLASH SONAR"

WITH ECHOLOCATION, the brain provides an alternative pathway for recreating visual representations of the physical world, using the auditory channel and sound waves to process visual information to navigate the environment. Auditory cues such as mouth clicks, cane tapping, and finger snapping provide the brain with another avenue for processing visual information, not much different from the way sonar works or the way bats perceive and navigate their environment. Daniel Kish, president of World Access for the Blind, describes the experience of processing information differently as seeing "flashes of sound" rather than "flashes of light," an ability he calls "flash sonar." "Flashes of sound" reminds me of McGurk's term "hearing lips," or Higashida's "What we're actually looking at is the other person's voice," each expression beautifully capturing the paradoxical nature of perception and the curious inner workings of the brain/mind.

In his TED talk, Daniel Kish describes his use of echolocation. He is also featured in a touching tribute to individuals who experience the world differently, in the music video for the X Ambassadors' song "Renegade," which can be found on YouTube.

ted.com/talks/daniel_kish_how_i_use_sonar_to_navigate_the_world

youtube.com/watch?v=1U-nilUB8HI

Daniel Kish also appears in a recent TVOntario documentary series called *Human Plus*, which investigates "the uptapped potential of sensory perception."

tvo.org/programs/human-plus

Neuroplasticity and Perception

When you get to the fork in the road, take it.

YOGI BERRA

Our growing understanding of the brain's wondrous ability to adapt and change itself offers an opportunity for us to think more deeply about individuals who follow the "road less travelled." In *The Brain That Changes Itself: Stories of Personal Triumph from the Frontiers of Science*, Norman Doidge (2007) documents the brain's fantastic ability to adapt when faced with challenging circumstances. The book's title reflects perfectly the neuroscience revealed by the McGurk effect, in which the brain appears to develop a neural pathway in order to establish an effective partnership between the visual and auditory modalities in the interest of efficient speech perception. This neural strategy or pathway—"if in doubt, look at the mouth"—begins to develop as typical infants mature and move through the stages of language acquisition and multi-sensory integration.

In describing *The Brain That Changes Itself*, Oliver Sacks writes, "Only a few decades ago, scientists considered the brain to be fixed or "hard-wired... Here [Doidge] describes in fascinating personal narratives how the brain, far from being fixed, has remarkable powers of changing its own structure and compensating for even the most challenging neurological conditions." Sacks also wrote about the importance of neuroplasticity and adaptive strategies as a means to unravelling the brain's ever-changing possibilities in the preface to his own book *An Anthropologist on Mars*, which takes its name from the chapter on Temple Grandin:

> This sense of the brain's remarkable plasticity, its capacity for the most striking adaptations, not least in the special (and often desperate) circumstances of neural and sensory mishap, has come to dominate my own perception of my patients and their lives. So much so, indeed, that I am sometimes moved to wonder whether it may not be necessary to redefine the very concepts of "health" and "disease," to see these in terms of the ability of the organism to create a new organization and order, one that fits its special, altered disposition and needs, rather than in terms of a rigidly defined "norm." (1996, xviii)

As we consider the various detours along the neuroplastic road, we might begin to realize that we are in fact more alike than different, for we all want to make sense of the world around us as best we can—easier for some, harder for others, but we are all on this road together. Individuals with sensory challenges may follow their own unique path to compensate for their deficits as they find a different way to connect to the world around them; for it is, as psycholinguistics pioneer Frank Smith (1971, ix) called it, the "human quality of language" that colours our perceptions and makes light visible within the spectrum of the mind's eye.

The Ends Justify the Means

Efficient speech perception is multisensory in nature, and the brain learns from experience that when processing language, other cues, like context, syntax, semantics, tone of voice, facial expressions, and body language, will help override any inaccuracies or misperceptions that may result from quickly integrating and processing all of the sensory information coming in; there is a certain linguistic redundancy built into language processing. Our brains have figured out that such inaccuracies or misperceptions, when experienced within in the context of meaningful language, are rather insignificant, since the other cueing systems will step in to right the wrong or alert us to the need for clarification. It is the multisensory and psycholinguistic aspects of language, with its built-in redundancy, and our neuroplastic capabilities that keep the wheels of speech perception turning.

When everything works together, all is well, but if the soundtrack seems misaligned with the picture, as in a poorly dubbed movie, perception can become a challenge. That may be how it feels for many individuals on the spectrum—except that instead of just watching a poorly dubbed film, they are actually a part of it as they try to make sense of all the conversational exchanges going on around them in their daily lives. It's not hard to imagine that trying to join such a conversation would feel awkward, frustrating, and overwhelming.

Thanks to the work of the researchers I've mentioned and many others, the important influence of the visual modality and the multisensory nature of speech perception can no longer be overlooked. Their findings serve to remind us of the influence of "hearing lips" and the need to rely on the mouth when sensory integration challenges present problems for individuals with ASD. Some individuals may become more reliant on watching the mouth as they try to follow conversations while continuing to work on integrating sight and sound more efficiently. Of course, this takes practice, and some need more time and practice than others. Some individuals may choose to look away when integration fails, as they try to figure out what is being said by simply listening. By choosing to process what is being said by using only the auditory modality, they are able to remove the overwhelming influence of other sources of information that they are not yet ready to process. Still others may develop traits like echolalia or hyperlexia.

Our wondrous brain offers many avenues for adapting to and perceiving the world around us. However, following the road less travelled, while fulfilling an important need, is not without its consequences, some serious and others less so, and those who follow a different path are often misunderstood. Neuroplasticity allows the brain to adapt when obstacles present themselves, revealing the intimate relationship between the mind and the various sensory receptors as they connect with the world around us.

More work is still needed, but at the very least the research to date has raised important questions that require us to reconsider what lies behind some of the characteristics of ASD, viewing them as more of a neurological response or consequence of managing sensory challenges than as a core social deficit. The adaptive strategies developed and used by individuals with ASD may now be viewed as reasonable responses on the part of the "thinking self" to help process language and the sensory world. So instead of just looking at the "acting self" that turns away and viewing this as a socially inappropriate response or a behavioural problem, perhaps we might now consider it as a way the "thinking self" has learned to compensate when struggling to process language toward better, not less, communication. Paradoxically, Ami Klin and colleagues (Klin et al. 2002) noted the presence of better social skills in individuals who look at the mouths of people speaking, which in itself suggests that we should rethink the way we introduce, integrate, and teach additional non-verbal social cues like eye contact while still maintaining the integrity of much-needed verbal cues like looking at the mouth. We need to carefully identify the importance of certain adaptive skills and build from there. To dismiss them out of hand may actually interfere with the acquisition of more highly developed skills.

The wheels within different kinds of minds are turning, but they've chosen to follow the road less travelled. Simply focusing on behaviours, without considering the individual adaptive strategies devised by the children themselves in order to process what is being communicated, may misdirect our attention and keep us from recognizing an important opportunity to improve speech and sensory integration and, above all, to find an opportunity for meaningful relationship.

Addressing the sensory issues that many believe lie at the core of ASD is long overdue. All development disorders point to a problem in development and skill acquisition. If we expect children with atypical development to be shoehorned into the typical developmental framework, we are limiting opportunities for growth. However, an appreciation for both typical and atypical development can help us chart a path toward a more nuanced integration of development, starting with the core sensory issues in concert with the learning strengths and styles of the individual. Working with autism, not against it, is a good place to begin.

Today the average person still intuitively assumes that speech perception is simply an auditory process, and many professionals and educators working in the field of ASD also hold on to this outdated view of speech perception when considering the needs of individuals on the spectrum. Perhaps this is because this view is more in keeping with the prevailing deficits view of ASD, where eye avoidance is mainly viewed from a social skills perspective while ignoring the well-established multimodal aspects of sight and sound as part of speech perception. This focus on eye avoidance has prevented many professionals from considering the speech perception avenue of inquiry when conducting assessments and from looking at the significant research that supports it.

When considering difficulties with communication disorders, using what we know about speech perception—and being aware of individualized sensory and learning style preferences—would certainly enhance the results of many of the excellent therapies currently in place. It is not enough to know that certain treatments work; we need to understand *why* they work. And for children who do not benefit from well-established treatments, knowing why there is a problem is equally valuable, for then we will know how to help them. Discovering more about what lies within different minds will allow us to help every child.

Conclusion
A Fish out of Water

I N THE 1980S, Albert Einstein became the poster boy for learning disabilities, and his inquisitive and expressive face was proudly displayed at many conferences. Today, when Temple Grandin speaks about autism spectrum disorder, she proudly includes him in her presentation. Einstein's association with these two different categories reminds me of one of Lorna Wing's last interviews, published in the *Guardian* (Rhodes 2011), in which she said she had come to believe that most people have some autistic traits: "I do believe you need autistic traits for real success in science and the arts, and I am fascinated by the behaviours and personalities of musicians and scientists."

It doesn't much matter whether Einstein was learning disabled, on the spectrum, a genius, all of the above, or somewhere in between. What we do know is that he possessed special traits of a unique mind. But what is also interesting is that in spite of his intellectual gifts, he did poorly in school; but he didn't let that get in the way of his education. How did he learn to compensate for his different learning style? In her book *Thinking in Pictures*, Grandin (2006, 212) wrote

Class is in Session

"Everybody is a genius. But if you judge a fish by its ability to climb a tree, it will live its whole life believing that it is stupid." – Albert Einstein

that Einstein told a psychologist friend, Max Wertheimer, that "thoughts did not come in any verbal formulation. I rarely think in words at all. A thought comes and I try to express it in words afterwards."

How many other unique students are failing because of the fixed mindsets of our educational system? I believe we have reached an important juncture in education and are finally beginning to see a shift—but so much more needs to be done. We are beginning to talk the talk, but many important changes need to take place before we can take the necessary steps to walk the walk. We are not there yet.

Today, students with learning disabilities are quite successful in the mainstream school system. Yet students on the spectrum who have a slightly different or more nuanced diagnosis continue to face the demands of a traditional system.

Their labels may be different, but they share unique and different learning styles. The focus should be not on labels but rather on education: what strengths and learning styles can we identify and how can we then provide a meaningful education plan to achieve the best possible outcome?

Eustacia Cutler, Temple Grandin's mother, has useful pointers that can help parents keep kindergarteners who learn differently in mainstream education. You can find her post on the website of the Temple Grandin & Eustacia Cutler Autism Fund.

templegrandineustaciacutlerautismfund. com/2019/06/23/i-want-my-child-in-regular-kindergarten-all-day

The confusion is understandable when we recognize the misunderstandings associated with labels and the way the terms are viewed and used by various stakeholders. Grandin (2013, 101-2) describes the view based on labels as "label-locked," because "people get so invested in what the word for the thing is that they no longer see the thing itself." In the teachers' handbook *Special Education in Ontario Schools*, the authors explain the problems associated with this type of thinking:

> After some four decades of in-depth experience, special education has yet to establish a set of clear, standardized categories and definitions that everyone accepts and uses. Part of the difficulty lies in the varying purposes of different stakeholders. Administrators use definitions for identifying candidates and for determining levels of support and resource allocation. Parents, advocates, and community

support associations, because they have more immediate remediation objectives, tend to emphasize extensive, symptom-based characteristics.

Some support groups argue for no definitions at all because students with special needs simply do not fit into such confines.

Other stakeholders have very individualistic perspectives. Medical professionals have their own view, one that often has limited connection with education. Researchers may develop their own definitions to limit the variables in a study. Teachers and educational assistants want definitions to provide a practical guidance point for planning and practice. Then there is the very notion of special need itself. To anyone who reflects on the fact that normalcy is not defined, it is no surprise that departure from normal is hard to describe. (Bennett, Dworet, and Weber 2013, 31–32)

Learning differently, regardless of the label, should be the primary focus of educators today. "Don't worry about the label," Grandin (2013, 105) wisely advises. "Tell me what the problem is. Let's talk about the specific symptoms."

It is curious that I now find myself advocating on behalf of my students with ASD and/or developmental differences in much the same way I did back in the 1970s for my students with learning disabilities. I've seen the important and successful shifts that have happened in the three decades since students like Anthony first introduced learning disabilities and learning differently to our educational system. Individualized education plans were just being developed at the time, and now they are common practice. I believe learning-style profiles should be developed for every student in their early years of school; again, this is simply teaching at its best. We are now challenged with extending what we already know to every unique mind.

The good news is that the learning disabilities legacy has taught us important lessons about people who learn differently. Differentiated instruction is now widely practiced. Teacher training now focuses on understanding dynamic differentiated learning styles; developing inclusive learning communities and bullying awareness is a common goal for education today.

Chantal Sicile-Kira, an excellent advocate as a parent, author, and professional, provides helpful information on post-secondary opportunities and career options for people on the spectrum through her organization, Autism College.

autismcollege.com

A new study has examined ways to prepare adults with autism for employment success. Find out more about it at the website of the Association for Science in Austism Treatment.

asatonline.org/research-treatment/clinical-corner/adults-employment-success

Yet "special" education is still considered as separate and apart and has not been wholly integrated into the educational psyche; there is still that sense of otherness, rather than of just being different, particularly for non-verbal and highly anxious students with ASD or students with physical challenges. We tend to underestimate students who may appear to be underachievers when in fact nothing could be further from the truth. We must raise our expectations, stretch students and teachers beyond their comfort zones, identify student strengths, and encourage them to use their skills to develop to their full potential. What holds us back is our difficulty with changing our perception of those who appear different. We are the ones who must change our behaviour and recognize our students' strengths and capabilities.

Our new task is to change our current mindset. Just as we rose to the challenge back in the 1970s, so too can we begin to extend our deep understanding of those who learn differently to all students.

EUSTACIA CUTLER

TEMPLE GRANDIN'S mother, Eustacia Cutler, forever changed our understanding of autism, offering new hope for families struggling to meet the needs of children no one understood. That journey began in the late 1940s when, as a young mother in "both years and experience" (2004, x), she single-handedly fought against the practice of institutionalizing "disturbed" children, choosing instead to keep her daughter at home and involved with family life, the community, and school. This wasn't easy in an era that blamed mothers for their children's autism.

Cutler's personal story forged a path for others to follow, and she never let go of hope as she continued to look for meaningful answers. In the 1960s, her research on autism and other developmental disabilities resulted in the production of two documentaries, one about what was then called mental retardation, entitled *The Innocent*, and the second about "disturbed" children, entitled *The Disquieted*. Over the course of her research, she visited a well-known psychiatric hospital with a residential unit for autistic children:

As long as I live I will never forget stepping off the elevator onto the floor of silent isolated children, each obsessed with some meaningless repetitive preoccupation... I search the faces of these withdrawn children in their silent Bedlam, this huge private playpen where no child plays with another, and wonder, is this another place Temple might have been sent? I think of Temple's nanny, her play sessions with Temple, her insistence that Temple be continually involved. I think of Mrs. Reynolds' speech classes and Mrs. Huckle's camp. It's the middle of the day, why aren't these children in some kind of school set-up? What therapy and/ or education are they receiving? (109–10)

Cutler's visit to the children's unit sounds eerily similar to Maria Montessori's visit to the asylum fifty years earlier. But Temple Grandin's mother had already discovered there was a better way and recognized that these children, like her daughter, needed "some kind of school set-up." According to Grandin (2013, 4), her mother "discovered on her own the standard treatment that therapists use today... the core principle of every program— including the one that was used with me, Miss Reynolds' Basement Speech-therapy School Plus Nanny—is to engage with the kid one-on-one for hours every day, 20 to 40 hours per week." Cutler does justice to the term *mother of invention*, as she set about discovering many of the best practices used in therapy programs today, along with recognizing the important role educa-tion and community life can have on children most in need of their benefits.

Today, Eustacia Cutler is in her nineties, still hard at work as she recognizes the continued need to advocate on behalf of families and their children with autism spectrum disorder. She is a popular international speaker, dedicated to promoting the latest research on the neurological nature of the autistic brain and its relation to neuroplasticity and the promise that such research has for helping more children develop their potential. Travelling is a little more difficult for her now, but a simple click will link you to Cutler's blog and free webinars. She will warmly welcome you into her New York City apartment, filled with the treasures gathered throughout a life enriched by her passions and challenges—a life that has included an eclectic career in theatre, earning a degree in English from Harvard, singing at New York's Pierre Hotel, and writing her life story, *A Thorn in My Pocket*. Her personal collection of books, art, photos, and memorabilia, assembled over many decades, serves to remind us of the message she continually shares with families—to remember who you are when facing life's twists and turns. Pursuing our passions and dreams will help shape our identities, and ground and sustain us both in good times and bad.

Eustacia Cutler and Temple Grandin have established the Temple Grandin & Eustacia Cutler Autism Fund (templegrandineustaciacutlerautismfund.com), dedicated to serving the needs of families and their children.

CUTLER 2004 Grandin and Panek 2013

Epilogue
In the Garden

Where you tend a rose, my lad, a thistle cannot grow.

FRANCES HODGSON BURNETT *The Secret Garden*

A S I WRITE the last pages of my book and think back to when I first began teaching, I know that we still have much to learn. But I am hopeful.

Buried Treasure

It was September when I arrived at my new school, about to meet my adolescent students with special needs for the first time. I parked my car and walked toward the back doors. I couldn't believe what I saw just outside my ground-floor classroom windows: a long-forgotten weedy patch of dirt with broken pickets, bits of paper, and old plastic bags from discarded lunches. What a mess—I couldn't believe my good luck!

I was new to the school and didn't feel comfortable staking out my territory just yet, but I had to claim that patch of weeds as soon as possible. After all, it was fall, a perfect time to start a garden and a perfect beginning to the new school year. I asked the principal if, with the help of my students, I might clear out the weeds and garbage in the back lot and maybe plant a few bulbs, which I would purchase myself. "No problem," he replied. "Nobody has worked in that old garden for years." And he kindly offered to help pay for some of the plantings. Let the digging begin.

This was also a perfect opportunity to introduce my new group of students to Frances Hodgson Burnett's children's classic *The Secret Garden*, which quickly became a classroom favourite. Just like the children in the novel, we too had discovered a secret garden in our own backyard and would begin our own transformation, as hidden treasures within ourselves were about to be discovered and realized. Old gardening and seed catalogues were soon cut up and turned into landscaping projects as we designed our dream garden. We had important work ahead and no time to waste. We couldn't wait to dirty our hands and reclaim this lost treasure.

The Secret Garden tells the story of two miserable ten-year-old cousins, a boy named Colin and a girl named Mary, who are abandoned to the care of servants in a rambling old country estate in Yorkshire, where they are kept apart and in the beginning are completely unaware of each other's existence. Colin is overly protected by the adults in his life, who believe he has a weak constitution and therefore must remain in bed; they indulge his alleged physical weaknesses and overlook his strengths, resigning him and those around him to a sense of hopelessness. Mary arrives at the estate following the death of her parents and is facing her own personal challenges.

Eventually the children find each other, and their lives are changed forever. Mary begins to discover friendship and joy for the first time in her life as she explores the grounds of the grand estate. Her curiosity leads her to discover the "invalid" Colin, who is confined to his bed. But she has no preconceived ideas about Colin's *dis*Ability and is having none of his negativity and resignation. She insists that he try to leave his bed and believes he "can do better." Soon they venture outside and begin to explore the secret garden, hidden from view behind a stone wall on the estate. Together, the children learn to overcome their weaknesses as they discover their own and each other's hidden strengths and gifts, which, like the secret garden, needed to be unearthed and nourished.

For these, the final pages of my book, I've borrowed the same title from the last chapter of *The Secret Garden* to honour its message of discovery and hope.

FRANCES HODGSON Burnett begins the chapter with a passage in which she cautiously reminds us of the power of ideas, attitudes, thoughts, and mindset, and the impact they can have on those around us—the very thing I've tried to demonstrate here. The passage brings to mind all of the educational visionaries I've respectfully referred to throughout this book:

> In each century since the beginning of the world wonderful things have been discovered. In the last century more amazing things were found out than in any century before. In this new century hundreds of things still more astounding will be brought to light. At first people refuse to believe that a strange new thing can be done, then they begin to hope it can be done, then they see it can be done—then it is done and all the world wonders why it was not done centuries ago. ([1911] 1997, 281)

As the students and I began to make plans for our new garden, they asked me how soon it would be until we had real flowers. I explained that all the fall bulbs we were planting would bloom in the spring—tulips, daffodils, allium, and hyacinths, and maybe some surprises, too, since the garden was overgrown and many hidden plants from past gardens might reappear. We would have to wait until the spring and see. But they insisted: "Can't we have flowers now and not have to wait until spring?" After all, they had worked so hard clearing the weeds, removing garbage, adding topsoil and mulch.

Of course, I agreed we needed flowers. I told them there was a wonderful flowering plant that blooms only in the fall. I explained that while most plants flower in spring and summer, we are lucky to have some "exceptional" plants that bloom much later and do not follow the "typical" growing season, and that this makes them especially precious and beautiful. "Mum's the word," I said. We would plant mums. They laughed and repeated, "Mum's the word... mums?" I explained that the flowers were called mums for short and sounded just like mum/mom for mother, but that the flower's full name was chrysanthemum.

Yes, I agreed, mums would be perfect in our garden.

AS I finish writing, I pause to look down at my own garden through the window above my desk, where I can see the last few blooms of my pink chrysanthemums. My students and I immediately connected with this late bloomer—the first flowers in our new garden would always be special to us.

"But why won't our mums bloom again in the spring with our other flowers?" they wondered.

As I searched for an answer, I remembered a long-forgotten poem that reminded me of the truth and beauty my students and I had discovered in our own secret garden that year. For when words fail, there's always poetry and the wonder of nature.

The Last Chrysanthemum
By Thomas Hardy

Why should this flower delay so long
To show its tremulous plumes?
Now is the time of plaintive robin-song,
When flowers are in their tombs.

Through the slow summer, when the sun
Called to each frond and whorl
That all he could for flowers was being done,
Why did it not uncurl?

It must have felt that fervid call
Although it took no heed,
Waking but now, when leaves like corpses fall,
And saps all retrocede.

Too late its beauty, lonely thing,
The season's shine is spent,

Nothing remains for it but shivering
In tempests turbulent.

Had it reason for delay,
Dreaming in witlessness
That for a bloom so delicately gay
Winter would stay its stress?

–I talk as if the thing were born
With sense to work its mind;
Yet it is but one mask of many worn
By the Great Face behind.

Notes

Introduction

1. In England and Wales, the Education (Handicapped Children) Act of 1971 stated that "all children... have become the responsibility of the education authorities" (L. Wing 1976, xi), moving "from the Health to the Education Service" (Elgar and Wing 1969, 15). Wing and Elgar wrote that "when this happens the differentiation of children into those 'suitable' and those 'not suitable' for education will no longer apply." The Federal Education for All Handicapped Children Act, later renamed the Individuals with Disabilities Education Act, was passed in the United States in 1975.

2. The term *learning disabilities* was first proposed in the 1960s by S. Kirk, former head of the American National Advisory Committee of Handicapped Children (Bennett, Dworet, and Weber 2013).

3. This sentiment was beautifully dramatized in a TVO video series based on the book *A Different Understanding: Learning Disabilities—What Do You Do with a Kid Like That?* (Toronto: TV Ontario Publications).

4. William Cruikshank was one of the first to recognize the neurological nature of learning and in 1946 envisioned special education as a distinct discipline, establishing the Department of Education for Exceptional Children at Syracuse University. In 1980 (103-11) he wrote:

   The interesting yet discouraging aspect to the situation is that since 1963, the neurophysiological aspects of the tremendous problem of learning disabilities have been essentially rejected by most parents and many educators... I suspect that this is the case because... so few psychologists and educators ever move into the basic sciences as an integral part of their preparatory training. Few in the field of learning disabilities... have studied in the area of neurophysiology, childhood psychopathology, anatomy, or neuropsychology. What one does not know, one tends to reject even though the unknown may be central to the problem...

[T]he fundamental basis for all learning and for the potential for mislearning is neurological... When one is faced by educators, psychologists, other professional persons, and parents who either deny the existence of the neurological component of the child's problem... then one fears for the future of the field as a whole and for the nature of the services which children are now receiving from well-intentioned but professionally ignorant people.

5. Over time, the definition of autism was still evolving, as shown by the expanding categories and criteria in each subsequent edition of the DSM. It was only in 1987 that "infantile autism" was changed to "autistic disorder," and since then we have seen the subsequent addition and removal of Asperger's syndrome. The most recent edition—the DSM-5, published in 2013—is quite good, with the important addition of sensory issues as a primary feature of ASD, along with the addition of Wing's long-overdue concept of autism as a spectrum. (For a more detailed account, see pp. 14–15 in Temple Grandin's *The Autistic Brain: Thinking across the Spectrum*, and for a more concise summary, see the autism timeline on p. 558 in John Donvan and Caren Zucker's *In a Different Key: The Story of Autism*).

6. Sheila Bennett, Don Dworet, and Ken Weber (2013, 26) define this as follows:

Universal Design for Learning encourages teachers to take the needs of all their students, whether academic, social, intellectual, or physical, into account when planning instruction. This consideration is to occur at the outset of planning, rather than making adjustments after the planning occurs, as has been traditionally done.

Differentiated classroom instruction… requires teachers to "begin where students are, not the front of the curriculum guide. They accept and build upon the premise that learners differ in important ways." Teachers following this approach begin their planning with the needs of all students in mind and present lessons and activities in a manner that effectively captures the needs and abilities of all students in their classrooms.

Some teacher preparation programs are trying to better prepare graduates to teach students with disabilities, especially in inclusion classrooms. At Syracuse University in upstate New York, George Theoharis, a professor and the chair of Teaching and Leadership, said the school's elementary special education program has been one of the leaders nationwide in training educators for inclusive education, noting that "regardless of what job teachers get, people need to be prepared to work with all children and see all children as their responsibility" (Mader 2017). For more, see disabilityscoop. com/2017/03/08/is-teacher-failing-disabilities/23421.

7. American parent activist Ruth Sullivan advocated for universal access to public education for special needs children in 1965. At the time, a reporter wrote a story about Sullivan's son Joe, whom he described as "a boy who was 'ready for school,' although 'school was not ready for him.'" John Donvan and Caren Zucker (2016, chapters 11-12) provide a full account of (and a beautiful tribute to) Ruth Sullivan's contribution to the field of ASD and her collaboration with Bernard Rimland in forming the still influential and important Autism Society of America (formerly the National Society for Autistic Children).

Chapter 1

1. The terms *idiot* and *feeble-minded* were in common use at the time. How interesting to note, however, that the term *feeble-minded* emphasizes weakness, but Montessori reframed this by seeing children's strengths. And keep in mind that it was not that long ago, when I started teaching, that terms like *ineducable* and *non-educable*

were commonly used, thereby determining future outcomes from the very beginning. Sadly, the lingering influence from that mindset continues to affect our understanding and expectations.

Chapter 3

1. Bruno Bettelheim, who actively promoted this view, was later discredited and lost his standing as a professional in the field of autism and child psychology. Temple Grandin (2013, 5–10) provides an excellent analysis, describing the faulty reasoning and confusion on the part of doctors like Kanner in the 1950s as they struggled to understand what might be causing this newly identified condition. The *Time* magazine article "Medicine: Frosted Children" (April 26, 1948; available at content.time.com/time/subscriber/article/ 0,33009,798484,00.html) popularized the notion of the "refrigerator mother": "The children, says Dr. Kanner, were 'kept neatly in a refrigerator which didn't defrost.'" Kanner later recanted this view and accepted the new organic theory of autism, being advocated by Rimland with whom he had regular correspondence. (Donovan and Zucker 2016, 118–19)

Chapter 5

1. Temple Grandin (2013, 18) has noted a serious problem regarding the impact of a typographical error in relation to PDD-NOS:

The number of diagnoses of autism spectrum disorder almost certainly went up dramatically for another reason, one that hasn't gotten as much attention as it should: a typographical error. Shocking but true. In the DSM-IV, the description of pervasive developmental disorder not otherwise specified that was supposed to appear in print was a "severe and pervasive impairment in social interaction *and* in verbal or non-verbal communication skills" (emphasis added). What actually appeared, was "a severe and pervasive impairment of reciprocal social interaction *or* verbal and non-verbal communication skills" (emphasis added). Instead of needing to meet *both* criteria to merit the diagnosis of PDD-NOS, a patient needed to meet either.

We can't know how many doctors made an incorrect diagnosis of PDD-NOS based on this error. The language was corrected in 2000 in the DSM-IV-TR. Even so, we can't know how many doctors continued to make the incorrect diagnosis, if only because by then the incorrect diagnosis had become the standard diagnosis.

In the DSM-5, published in 2013, PDD-NOS has been removed.

Chapter 6

1. An official English translation would not be available until 1991. Uta Frith's translation, "'Autistic Psychopathy' in Childhood," in *Autism and Asperger Syndrome,* edited by Frith (the original appeared as Asperger's "Die autistischen psychopathen im kindesalter" in *Archiv für Psychiatrische und Nervenkrankheiten* 117 [1944: 76–136]), would eventually introduce the rest of the English-speaking world to the work of Hans Asperger and "autistic psychopathy" or, as it later became known, Asperger syndrome. This syndrome would eventually broaden the spectrum even further.

2. A recent shift in mindset is reflected in the DSM-5 (2013), where the more general term Autism Spectrum Disorder replaced the earlier DSM-IV subsets—autistic disorder, Asperger's disorder, childhood disintegrative disorder, and PDD-NOS (Pervasive Development Disorder–Not Otherwise Specified). According to the National Autistic Society (Ayris 2013, 33–34), "the revisions to DSM-5 mean that when people go for a diagnosis in the future, instead of receiving a diagnosis of one of these disorders, they will be given a diagnosis of autism spectrum disorder (ASD) ... The emphasis during diagnosis will change from giving a name to the condition to identifying all the needs a person has. 'Dimensional elements' have been introduced which give an indication of how much someone's condition affects them. This will help to identify the support that the person might need."

Chapter 7

1. Priscilla Gilman also published a book about her son, entitled *The Anti-Romantic Child: A Memoir of Unexpected Joy* (2011).
2. For a wonderful account of the Bletchley group and one code cracker in particular, called the Lady of the Lake, see William Stevenson's *A Man Called Intrepid* (1977).

Chapter 10

1. This hope was described as a "pivotal response" by Eric Schopler, one of the founders of the TEACCH program, in his chapter, "Towards Reducing Behavior Problems in Autistic Children" (1976, 229), in Lorna Wing's book *Early Childhood Autism*:

> From a behaviorist position it is natural to be searching for and hoping to tap a "pivotal response" in the autistic child, an "intervening variable," which when modified will improve a host of other functions. If you could teach the child normal eye contact, he might become related, learn to talk, and so on. The disappointment in not finding behavior leading to a "pivotal response" was eloquently documented by Lovaas (1973). This inclination to formulate a technique that will cure or help all autistic children is pursued by many professionals and many such techniques are found in the clinical marketplace, from megavitamins to electronic typewriters. All of them reported some success, none of them for all autistic children. This lack of success in "curing" autistic children should surprise no one. The level of intelligence and degree and extent of impairment are not the same for all these children. Their individual differences are more impressive than their similarities. There is in fact no more basis for employing such a tactic as the "pivotal response" than there is for claiming the possibility for an exclusive and totally successful rehabilitative technique. Many professionals have fallen into this trap. If they stumble on a technique that helps one child, they feel they have not played their social role unless other autistic children can be made to fit their treatment techniques.

2. Sir Michael Rutter, the first child psychiatrist in the UK and an expert on autism, stated back in 1969 in his preface to Elgar and Wing's booklet, *Teaching Autistic Children*, "The exact nature of

the communications difficulty is unknown but it seems that it may be related to a defect in the brain's 'processing' of information it receives from the senses, perhaps especially when the information involves symbols (such as in language). It is probable that to a considerable extent, the social problems stem from this defect. This view has obvious implications for treatment."

References

Abramson, Keren, Paula Aquilla, Lynda Beedham, et al. n.d. Resource booklet originally published by the now defunct Canadian Hyperlexia Association.

Adams, Marilyn Jager. 1991. *Beginning to Read: Thinking and Learning about Print*. Cambridge, MA: The MIT Press.

American Psychiatric Association. 1980. *The Diagnostic and Statistical Manual of Mental Disorders* III. Washington, DC.

———. 1994. *The Diagnostic and Statistical Manual of Mental Disorders* IV. Washington, DC.

———. 2000. *The Diagnostic and Statistical Manual of Mental Disorders* IV-TR. Washington, DC.

———. 2013. *The Diagnostic and Statistical Manual of Mental Disorders* 5. Washington, DC.

Asperger, Hans. 1944. "Die autistischen psychopathen im kindesalter." *Archiv für Psychiatrische und Nervenkrankheiten* 117: 76–136.

Attwood, Tony. 2007. *The Complete Guide to Asperger's Syndrome*. London: Jessica Kingsley Publishers.

Autism Speaks Canada. n.d. The Early Start Denver Model. autismspeaks.ca.

Autism UK Independent. n.d. "Teacch Programme." autismuk.com/training/teacch-programme.

Ayris, Elizabeth. 2013. "What's in a Name?" *Your Autism Magazine*, Autumn 2013.

Barnett, Kristine. 2013. *The Spark: A Mother's Story of Nurturing Genius*. Toronto: Vintage Canada.

Bennett, Sheila, and Don Dworet, with Ken Weber. 2013. *Special Education in Ontario Schools*, 7th ed. St. Davids, Ontario: Highland Press.

Bennett, Sheila, Don Dworet, Tiffany L. Gallagher, and Monique Somma. 2019. *Special Education in Ontario Schools*, 8th ed. St. Davids, Ontario: Highland Press.

Blake, Quentin Sir. 2015. *Tell Me a Picture*. London: National Gallery.

Brugha, Traolach S., et. al. 2011. "Legacy of John Wing 1923-2010." *British Journal of Psychiatry* (February): 176-78.

Burnett, Frances Hodgson. (1911) 1997. *The Secret Garden*. New York: Scholastic.

Canadian Hyperlexia Association. n.d. *Hyperlexia* (fact sheet). judyanddavid.com/cha/whatishyperlexia.pdf.

Carey, Benedict. 2006. "Bernard Rimland, 78, Scientist Who Revised View of Autism, Dies." *New York Times*, November 28.

Chabris, Christopher, and Daniel Simons. 2010. *The Invisible Gorilla and Other Ways Our Intuitions Deceive Us*. New York: Crown.

Colasent, Rita, and Penny L. Griffith. 1998. *The Reading Teacher 51 (5)*. Hoboken: Wiley.

Cruikshank, William. 1980. "Learning Disabilities: Perceptual or Other?" In *A Different Understanding: Learning Disabilities*, edited by Patricia Thorvaldson, 101-11. Toronto: TVO Publications.

Cutler, Eustacia. 2004. *A Thorn in My Pocket: Temple Grandin's Mother Tells the Family Story*. Arlington, TX: Future Horizons.

Diament, Michelle. 2015. "Schools Favor Inclusion When Forced to Report Academic Progress." *Disability Scoop*. disabilityscoop. com/2015/02/13/schools-inclusion-report/20060.

Doerr, Anthony. 2014. *All the Light We Cannot See*. New York: Scribner.

Doidge, Norman. 2007. *The Brain That Changes Itself: Stories of Personal Triumph from the Frontiers of Science*. New York: Penguin.

Donvan, John, and Caren Zucker. 2016. *In a Different Key: The Story of Autism*. New York: Crown.

Elgar, Sybil. 1969. "Appendix: Seven Autistic Children." *Early Childhood Autism: Clinical, Educational and Social Aspects*, edited by John Wing. Oxford, UK: Pergamon Press.

Elgar, Sybil, and Lorna Wing. 1969. *Teaching Autistic Children: Guide Lines for Teachers 5*. London: College of Special Education and National Society for Autistic Children.

Feinstein, Adam. 2001. "Interview with Professor Gary Mesibov." *Looking Up* 2 (10). lookingupautism.org/articles/garymesibov.html.

———. 2010. *A History of Autism: Conversations with the Pioneers.* Chichester, UK: Wiley-Blackwell.

Frith, Uta. 1991. "'Autistic Psychopathy' in Childhood." In *Autism and Asperger Syndrome*, edited by Uta Frith, 37–92. Cambridge: Cambridge University Press.

Gilman, Priscilla. 2011. *The Anti-Romantic Child: A Memoir of Unexpected Joy.* New York: Harper Collins.

———. 2013. "Early Reader." *New York Times*, August 25. nyti.ms/13UmHFv.

Golick, Margie. 1973. *Deal Me In! The Use of Playing Cards in Teaching and Learning.* Guilford, CT: Jeffrey Norton.

Goodman, K. 2001. *On Reading.* Portsmouth, NH: Heinemann.

Gould, Judith. 2014. "Lorna Wing." *Guardian*, June 22.

Grace, Fiona. 2018. "Lorna Wing: An Autism Hero." *Your Autism Magazine* (Winter).

Grandin, Temple. 2006. *Thinking in Pictures: My Life with Autism.* New York: Vintage.

———. 2008. *The Way I See It: A Personal Look at Autism and Asperger's.* Arlington, TX: Future Horizons.

Grandin, Temple, and Catherine Johnson. 2010. *Animals Make Us Human: Creating the Best Life for Animals.* New York: Houghton Mifflin Harcourt.

Grandin, Temple, and Margaret Scariano. 2005. *Emergence: Labeled Autistic.* New York: Grand Central Publishing.

Grandin, Temple, and Richard Panek. 2013. *The Autistic Brain: Thinking across the Spectrum.* New York: Houghton Mifflin Harcourt.

Grant, Tavia. 2015. "Working Wisdom: How People with Disabilities Give Companies an Edge." *Globe and Mail*, February 27. theglobeandmail.com/report-on-business/working-wisdom-how-workers-with-disabilities-give-companies-an-edge/article23236023.

Hall, Elaine. 2015. "Heroes Among Us: Dr. Barry Prizant." *Huffington Post*, August 6. huffpost.com/entry/heroes-among-us-dr-barry_b_7923008.

Hall, Elaine, and Dianne Isaacs. 2012. *Seven Keys to Unlock Autism.* San Francisco: Jossey-Bass.

Higashida, Naoki. 2013. *The Reason I Jump: The Inner Voice of a Thirteen-Year-Old Boy with Autism.* New York: Random House.

Jones, Warren, and Ami Klin. 2013. "Attention to Eyes Is Present but in Decline in 2-6-Month-Olds Later Diagnosed with Autism." In *Nature* 504 (December 19): 427–31.

Kanner, Leo. 1943. "Autistic Disturbances of Affective Contact." In *Nervous Child* 2: 217–50.

Klin, Ami, Warren Jones, Robert Schultz, Fred Volkmar, and Donald Cohen. 2002. "Defining and Quantifying the Social Phenotype in Autism." In *American Psychiatry* 159 (6): 895–908.

Kluth, Paula. n.d. Paula Kluth News (newsletter). paulakluth.com

Kluth, Paula, and Kelly Chandler-Olcott. 2008. *A Land We Can Share: Teaching Literacy to Students with Autism.* Baltimore: Brookes Publishing.

Koch, Kenneth. 1974. *Rose, Where Did You Get That Red? Teaching Great Poetry to Children.* New York: Random House.

Kupperman, Phyllis. 2017. *The Source: Intervention in Autism Spectrum Disorders,* 2nd ed. Austin: Pro-Ed.

Mader, Jackie. 2017. "Is Teacher Preparation Failing Students with Disabilities?" *The Hechinger Report,* March 8.

McGurk, Harry, and John MacDonald. 1976. "Hearing Lips and Seeing Voices" (letter to the editor). In *Nature* 264: 746–48.

Mesibov, Gary B., Victoria Shea, Eric Schopler. 2004. *The TEACCH Approach to Autism Spectrum Disorders.* New York: Springer.

Mill, John Stuart. 1860. "Thoughts on Poetry and Its Varieties." In *The Crayon* 7 (4): 93–97.

Miller, Susan M. 1993. *Reading Too Soon.* Center for Speech and Language Disorders.

Montessori, Maria. (1912) 1964. *The Montessori Method.* New York: Schocken Books.

Moriuchi, Jennifer M., Ami Klin, and Warren Jones. 2017. "Mechanisms of Diminished Attention to Eyes in Autism." In *American Journal of Psychiatry* 74 (1): 26–35.

Prizant, Barry. 2015. *Uniquely Human: A Different Way of Seeing Autism.* New York: Simon & Schuster.

Prizant, Barry, Amy Wetherby, Emily Rubin, Amy Laurent, and Patrick Rydell. 2005. *The SCERTS Model: A Comprehensive Educational Approach for Children with Autism Spectrum Disorders.* Baltimore: Brookes Publishing.

Research Autism. 2016. "Research Autism to Address the Toxic Effects of Stress for Autistic People and Their Families." researchautism.net/about-us-research-autism/beating-stress-in-autism.

Rhodes, Giulia. 2011. "Autism: A Mother's Labour of Love." *Guardian*, May 24.

Rich, Nathaniel. 2015. "A Training Ground for Artists." *New York Times*, December 16. nytimes.com/2015/12/20/magazine/a-training-ground-for-untrained-artists.html.

Rimland, Bernard. (1964) 2015. *Infantile Autism: The Syndrome and Its Implications for a Neural Theory of Behavior*. London and Philadelphia: Jessica Kingsley Publishers.

Roberts, Wendy. 2006. "Redefining Autism." *National Post*, October 9.

Rogers, Sally. 2015. Keynote speech at European Society for Child and Adolescent Psychiatry conference, Madrid. escap.eu.

Rogers, Sally J., Geraldine Dawson, Laurie A. Vismara. 2012. *An Early Start for Your Child with Autism*. New York: Guilford Press.

Sacks, Oliver. 1996. *An Anthropologist on Mars: Seven Paradoxical Tales*. Toronto: Vintage Canada.

Sales, Ben. 2015. "Soldiers with Autism Take on Key Roles in Israeli Military." *Forward*, December 13. forward.com/news/breaking-news/326511/deciphering-satellite-photos-soldiers-with-autism-take-on-key-roles-in-idf.

Schopler, Eric. (1976) 1980. "Towards Reducing Behaviour Problems in Autistic Children." In *Early Childhood Autism*, 2nd ed. with minor corrections, edited by Lorna Wing, 221–45.

Shattock, Paul. 2006. "Parent and Practitioner Revolutionizing the Treatment of Autism." *Guardian*, December 6.

Siegel, Bryna. 1996. *The World of the Autistic Child: Understanding and Treating Autistic Spectrum Disorders*. New York: Oxford University Press.

Siegel, Bryna. (2003) 2007. *Helping Children with Autism Learn: Treatment Approaches for Parents and Professionals*. Oxford and New York: Oxford University Press.

———. 2008. *Getting the Best for Your Child with Autism: An Expert's Guide to Treatment*. New York: Guilford Press.

Silberman, Steve. 2015. *NeuroTribes: The Legacy of Autism and Future of the Future of Neurodiversity*. New York: Avery.

Smith, Frank. 1971. *Understanding Reading: A Psycholinguistic Analysis of Reading and Learning to Read*. New York: Holt, Rinehart and Winston.

Standing, E.M. 1962. *Maria Montessori: Her Life and Work.* New York: New American Library.

Stevenson, William. 1977. *A Man Called Intrepid.* New York: Ballantine Books.

Suskind, Ron. 2014. *Life Animated.* Los Angeles and New York: Kingswell.

——. 2014. "Reaching My Autistic Son through Disney." *New York Times*, March 7. nytimes.com/2014/03/09/magazine/reaching-my-autistic-son-through-disney.html.

Telegraph. 2014. "Lorna Wing—Obituary." June 9.

Temple Grandin & Eustacia Cutler Autism Fund. 2015. *A Look at the History of Autism* over the Last 65 Years. Conversation with Dr. Gary Mesibov. Webinar, November 13. youtube.com/watch?v=QiK1PRO7r5A.

——. 2017. *Readings with Eustacia Cutler: Welcome to Limbo.* Video, April 25. youtube.com/watch?v=u6M2Hnoks80&t=15s.

Thorvaldson, Patricia, ed. *A Different Understanding: Learning Disabilities. What Do You Do with a Kid like That?* Toronto: TV Ontario Publications.

Times London. 2014. "Lorna Wing: Psychiatrist Whose Work Did Much to Improve the Understanding of Autism after Her Only Child Had Condition Diagnosed." June 12.

Treffert, Darold. 1990. *Extraordinary People: Understanding Savant Syndrome.* New York: Ballantine Books.

——. 2012. *Islands of Genius: The Bountiful Mind of the Autistic, Acquired, and Sudden Savant.* Philadelphia: Jessica Kingsley Publishers.

Treffert, Darold, Karen Bartelt, Beth Dardis, and Bryan Mischler. n.d. *Hyperlexia Manual: A Guide to Children Who Read Early.* Fond du Lac, WI: Treffert Center.

Wells, P. 2013. "Boy Genius." *Macleans,* September 9.

Wing, John, ed. (1966) 1969. *Early Childhood Autism: Clinical, Educational and Social Aspects.* Oxford, UK: Pergamon Press.

Wing, Lorna. 1972. *Autistic Children: A Guide for Parents and Professionals.* Seacaucus, NJ: Citadel Press.

——. 1976. *Early Childhood Autism: Clinical, Education and Social Aspects,* 2nd ed. Oxford, UK: Pergamon Press.

——. 1979. "The Current Status of Childhood Autism." In *Psychological Medicine* 9: 9–12.

———. 1981. "Asperger's Syndrome: A Clinical Account." In *Psychological Medicine* 11 (1): 115-29.

———. 1996. *The Autistic Spectrum: A Guide for Parents*. London: Constable.

———. 2001. *The Autistic Spectrum: A Parent's Guide to Understanding and Helping Your Child*. Berkeley: Ulysses Press.

———. 2006. *What's So Special about Autism?* London: National Autistic Society.

———. 2007. "Sybil Elgar." *Guardian*, January 24.

———. 2011. "John Wing's Life." In *British Journal of Psychiatry* 198 (3): 176-78.

Wing, Lorna, and Judith Gould. 1979. "Severe Impairments of Social Interaction and Associated Abnormalities in Children: Epidemiology and Classification." In *Journal of Autism and Developmental Disorders* 9 (1): 11-29.

Acknowledgements

'D LIKE TO thank the families, friends, educators, professionals and students who taught me how to stretch the boundaries of possibilities. Presented in chronological order, from my early years until the present:

Mrs. Young, my Grade 2 teacher, who encouraged me to exceed expectations and discover my spark for learning. Corinne Gross, who in 1973 established the first Ontario Society for Autistic Children in response to her own experiences with her son, Adam. And to Adam, who was just another kid on the block, who loved playing street hockey with us but wasn't able to join us at our neighbourhood school. Helen Honickman, a family friend, who first recruited me as a young girl to volunteer at an organization for children with intellectual disabilities. She later played an active role in supporting Famous People Players, a nonprofit black-light puppetry theatre company based in Toronto, featuring performances by a troupe of special needs individuals who tour around the world. And York University Faculty of Education professor Doreen Kronick, founder of Integra and Camp Towhee—organizations established in the 1970s that focused on enhancing the strengths and social lives of children (and later adults) with special needs.

Family court judge and child advocate Warren Durham, and Jeffery Wilson, lawyer and founding member of Justice for Children. The Peel Board of Education, which took on the challenge of special needs students in the late 1970s, and the teachers and professionals who became leaders in the field—Bill Quance, Radha Ahuja, John Amon, Chris Worsnop, Elsabeth Hanan, Lois Bedard, Pauline Auty, Alan Pleasance, Kathy O'Marra, Sheila Grupp, Pat Noble, and many more. Assistant dean Robert C. Barnett in the Faculty of Education at Nipissing University College, and their outreach summer programs, where I taught a special education summer course in the early 1980s. Debbie Wales, a teacher in my class, became a leader in special education for the Haliburton Board of Education. And to the educators at the City Adult Learning Centre, Toronto Board of Education, who advanced the educational needs of adults with exceptionalities and/or disabilities and helped them earn a high school diploma— until the special education supports were withdrawn in the late 1990s: Marnie Taylor, Nikki Fennel, Margaret Roddy, Carrie Hilhorst, Gord Baricevic, Mary Campbell, Dan Israel, Marianne Wollison, and many others. And to the high school teachers, educators, and support staff in both academic and special needs settings who went out of their way to encourage and support their students with exceptionalities: Linda Jones, June Gooding, Mary Card, Connie Kusel, Tanaz Anklesaria, Dan Retson, Cynthia Abernethy, Steve Yee, Laura Houghton, Jay Arrington, Derek Hayes, Elliot Scolnik, Snezana Radan, Alexis Devasahayam, Ellen Little, Roberta Anderson, Tamara Hrycak, Diane Miadovnik, Anu Sepp, Nancy Lee, Katherine Cowan, Alex Herreria, Celene Grossman, Cali Grossman, Patrick Likuski, Duncan Anderson, Ralph and Kitty Wintrob, and Karen Goldenberg (Jewish Vocational Services).

The ISAND team (Integrated Services for Autism and Neurodevelopmental Disorders, Toronto, Ontario), including Wendy Roberts, Candace Yantyshyn, and Barri Trager. Holland Bloorview Kids Rehabilitation Hospital, Surrey Place, the Reena Foundation, Geneva Centre for Autism, DANI Centre (Developing and Nurturing Independence), and TVOntario, dedicated to promoting the educational needs of all students. Carol Woodward Ratzlaff and Brad Ratzlaff and the Viva Youth Singers of Toronto, where "each voice matters." Abe Fuks and Salvatore and Diane Guerrera of Montreal, who continue to advocate for the diverse needs of children with exceptionalities. And to the leaders in the field of autism who took the time to offer guidance and suggest helpful resources: Temple Grandin and Cheryl Miller, Darold Treffert, Vivian Hazell, and the rest of the team of professionals at the Treffert Center; Ami Klin, Phyllis Kupperman, Paula Kluth, and Jennifer Krumins.

To the friends, parents and colleagues who have encouraged me during the writing of this book: Julie Schwartz, Helene Smagala, Janice Karlinsky, Myra Sourkes and Richard Lewin, Louise Lewin, Mae Lagartos, Gorett Reis, Deborah Sheppard, Barbara Sourkes, Stacey Levine, Patty Stewart, Leslie Warren, Tessa and Laurence Spero, Kara Cathcart, Candy Burstyn, Marilyn Biderman, Norman Doidge and Karen Lipton-Doidge and family, Wodek Szemberg and Estera Bekier, Sara Usher, Joseph and Sue Fernando, Alma Petchersky and Alex Tarnopolsky, Charles Hanly and Margaret-Ann Fitzpatrick Hanly, Elizabeth Young Bruehl, Alan and Susie Tenenhouse, Raisel Candib, Dorothy Candib and Ed Engel, Billy Shaffir, Howard Spring and Shelley Kirsch, Freema and Joe Trager, Susan Levitt, Ron Biderman, Tori Whillier, Wayne and Gita Whillier, Arthur and Bonnie Fish,

Ali Wasserman, Cindy Kirsh, Patti Thorlakson, Alison and Sean Armstrong, Rob and Nada Beamish, Martina and Rainer Winkelmann, Arlene Davis, Lorraine Balshin, David and Jennifer Levine, Hesh Troper, Holly Bick and Michael Wolfish, Julie Bick and Bernard Lewis, Cheryl Wetstein, Mindy Skapinker, Paula Draper, Michael Levin, Andrea Knight, Bev Reisman, and Colleen Craig. And to Maribeth Solomon and Lenny Solomon for deepening my appreciation of music.

Thank you to my publisher, Trena White, and her team of professionals at Page Two, Caela Moffet, and Jessica Werb Rony Ganon. A special thank you to my editors, Merrie-Ellen Wilcox and Melissa Edwards.

I am especially grateful to my husband, Cyril, who encouraged me to write this book. And to our children and grandchildren, who continue to challenge us to learn more about our hidden potential and what is possible.

About
the Author

AFTER MANY YEARS of working as a high school English teacher and special educator, Corinne Levitt decided to change direction and work primarily with adolescents with special needs and developmental differences. She wrote this book in recognition of the need to promote the important role an enriched educational experience can have on the lives of students who stand to benefit the most from best educational practices. Her background in learning disabilities, psycholinguistics, and the arts enabled her to "teach to the talent" while encouraging her students to discover and explore their potential. Now in retirement, she is a member of the VIVA Youth Singers and sings alongside many of her former students who encouraged her to discover her voice. Corinne has four adult children and four grandchildren, and lives with her husband in Toronto, Canada, where she was born and raised.

About the Artists

Eric Lewin and his younger brother David attended Corinne's high school for students with special needs. Now young adults, they have benefitted greatly from gifted and creative professionals who search for potential and are not discouraged by challenges. When he and his brother were asked to contribute artwork for the book cover, Eric exclaimed: "An art commission!" Taking the suggestion of the theme of fall gardens and Corinne's favourite flower, chrysanthemums, they worked on the project with their art teacher, Goret Reis, whose input was invaluable. She showed them how to look and how to see, and they were completely engaged in the process. Eric enjoys learning about great art, especially the Impressionists, and he painted his version of Monet's *Bed of Chrysanthemums*. David carefully studied photos of their school garden and images from the internet as models. Each of their paintings reflects their skill sets and personalities. They are honoured and proud to have contributed to the book.